Praise for
CONSUMER.OLOGY

CONSUMER.OLOGY

The Market Research Myth, the Truth about Consumers and the Psychology of Shopping

PHILIP GRAVES

NICHOLAS BREALEY
PUBLISHING

To my father, Ray, who encouraged me to think.

First published by
Nicholas Brealey Publishing in 2010

3-5 Spafield Street
Clerkenwell, London
EC1R 4QB, UK
Tel: +44 (0)20 7239 0360
Fax: +44 (0)20 7239 0370

20 Park Plaza, Suite 1115A
Boston
MA 02116, USA
Tel: (888) BREALEY
Fax: (617) 523 3708

www.nicholasbrealey.com
www.philipgraves.net

© Philip Graves 2010

Library of Congress Cataloging-in-Publication Data

Graves, Philip.
  Consumer.ology : the market research myth, the truth about consumers and
the psychology of shopping / Philip Graves.
      p. cm.
  Includes bibliographical references and index.
  ISBN 978-1-85788-550-7
  1. Consumer behavior. 2. Consumers--Research. 3. Marketing research. I.
Title. II. Title: Consumerology. III. Title: Consumer dot ology.
  HF5415.32.G73 2010
  658.8'34--dc22

                                                              2010015569

ISBN 978-1-85788-550-7

British Library Cataloguing in Publication Data
A catalogue record for this book is available from the
British Library.

Printed in Finland by WS Bookwell.

CONTENTS

"If I'd asked people what they wanted, they would have said a faster horse."

—Henry Ford

"It is as though reflecting on the reasons for our actions can prompt us to include stray, misleading, and nonoptimal information in our postaction assessments of why we have done things. We become less true to ourselves and also to the unconscious realities that led to our behavior in the first place."

—Daniel M. Wegner

"We're not aware of changing our minds even when we do change our minds. And most people, after they change their minds, reconstruct their past pinion—they believe they always thought that."

—Daniel Kahneman

FOREWORD
by KEVIN HOGAN

It begins with considering someone's past choices...

"Why did you go and do that?"
"I don't know!"
"What were you thinking?"
"I was hoping...

(or some other on-the-spot confabulation or after-the-fact rationalization is constructed here)

...that XYZ was going to happen."

And then there is the prediction of future behavior...

"Would you buy this product, if it were in the store?"
"Yes, it would be great! I love it."
"If we offered this service would you buy it?"
"Definitely."

When looking at the future, people have almost no fortune-telling
ability as to how they will behave or what they might or might not
buy. Furthermore, they certainly can't accurately tell you "why"
they did something in the past.

Now you don't have to ask.

The human brain operates on a system of "short cuts" and
"rules of thumb." Without these corner-cutting decision-making
tools we'd never get anything done in life. And because of the same
neural wiring, we often get ourselves in a heap of trouble doing
some incredibly foolish things.

Throughout human behaviors there are dozens of types of short cuts in decision making that help you know what people will do in the future. You can also pretty much know "why" people did things in the past without asking them.

And for businesses which need to bring profitable products and services to market, they never have to burn good money on focus groups, which have a horrible track record for predicting future results of behavior for most types of products and services.

Philip Graves has put together an excellent guide to understanding how to know what people will and won't do. He'll show you why people did things in the past that made "no sense" at all, both in retrospect and in real time.

I've studied consumer behavior for two decades and have concluded that there is a profitable and useful way to navigate the very expensive waters of product testing and understanding the drives and emotions behind the rationale and thinking of consumers' decision making.

Now you can have the benefit of years of knowledge and experience distilled into an easy-to-read and understand book... which, by the way, was a very good decision to buy!

How do I know that?

You'll find the answer to that question shortly.

Kevin Hogan
Minneapolis, MN
April 2010

OVERTURE

The moment of truth

Market research emerged during the media and advertising boom of the 1950s, when an understandable desire to know who was listening to or watching a particular program evolved into a desire to know what those people thought. "This seems useful," these new market researchers thought, "if we just ask them people will tell us what they want, what they like, and what they think. All we have to do then is do whatever they say. Great!" You can see how stressed executives would be grateful to hear that corporate decision making was about to get a whole lot easier.

Either by asking a few hundred people to complete a questionnaire or taking a far smaller number and really grilling them, the theory goes that useful, dependable insights can be garnered in this way. But are we looking for answers in the wrong place? After all, it wouldn't be the first time people have been seduced by the idea of a convenient solution that turned out to be no such thing.

Examples of our capacity for misplaced beliefs are not hard to find. If something *seems* plausible, impresses us, fits with what we'd like to think, or has been sold to us persuasively, we are willing to treat it as a truth. To compound the problem, the lines between science and belief are frequently blurred: elements of dependable science are blended with wishful thinking to create an alluring cocktail of reality and desirable fantasy. Astrologers get to lean on the legitimate science of astronomy and overlay bogus futurology to "help" people make decisions about their life (or in the case of Nancy Regan, her presidential husband's country). But such pseudo science, despite its masquerade, is no more dependable or repeatable than any other nonscientific belief. When astrologers' predictions are evaluated objectively, it transpires that nothing happened that can't be better credited to something other than the mystic force suggested by its exponents.

So where does market research sit on the scientific spectrum? Are opinion polls, focus groups, depth interviews, brand trackers, customer satisfaction questionnaires, online surveys and the like scientifically verifiable or are they used on the basis of faith? It may surprise you to learn that any market research that asks people what they think, what they've done, or what they would like in the future is based on belief. Market research is a pseudo science – in fact it's *consumer.ology* – and the beliefs underpinning it are false.

There are any number of accounts of where market research has been wrong. Products like Baileys liqueur that were rejected by consumers but launched anyway because of one senior manager's gut feel. Innovative concepts like the original Chrysler minivan and Compaq's PC network servers, that were developed despite what consumers said because someone in the organization appreciated how they would change an aspect of people's lives. The research for a new mobile phone that concluded few customers would buy it, but it outsold the resulting estimates by a factor of ten. Advertising like the *Heineken refreshes the parts...* campaign that research respondents said they didn't like but, when someone convinced the company to use it in any case, went on to be massively successful. And opinion polls like the ones looking at what should happen to a portion of the BBC licence fee – one concluded that 66% of people supported the government's preferred option, another just 6%!

In the past few decades we have started to learn a lot from science about how people think. Neuroscientists can see which areas of the brain are involved during different mental and physical activities, and psychologists have tested how various stimuli and interactions change how people behave. Their work helps explain what some marketing experts have known intuitively for some time: that successful marketing must connect with emotions if it is to succeed. As you will see in Chapter 2, several factors influence what we feel before we are consciously aware of our own actions; even after we act, we remain unaware of how each of these has shaped our behavior. Psychology and neuroscience have discovered that we're all rather bad at explaining our actions, as we are at predicting what we want or what we will do in the future. As

Timothy D. Wilson, psychology professor at the University of Virginia, puts it in the title of his book, we are *Strangers to Ourselves*. And the way in which we can be influenced without realizing that our thoughts have changed, while more than a little disconcerting, reveals what is required if understanding what people think is important to you *and* why the research process is frequently the cause of its own inaccuracy.

In just half a century, the rise of market research has been meteoric: in the US the market is worth over $11 billion and in the UK more than £1.3 billion is spent each year. Just one research study by the UK Department of Health cost more than £11 million![1] Organizations have been seduced by the numerology of statistics and the apparent consistency of response that market research provides. The elegant, scientifically demonstrable, statistical techniques for summarizing data sets provide enormous reassurance; after all, few things are more definitive than a number. When the number is obtained several times over, or when the groups of people interviewed in depth reach a clear consensus, it feels as though something true has been uncovered. But when the answers being summarized are spurious, the statistical confidence that can be attributed to them is an irrelevance. Yes, repeated studies might produce similar results, but that doesn't mean that the original results are accurate. The fact that people react similarly to consistently executed questioning processes doesn't tell us anything other than that the cause-and-effect relationship of such research is consistent.

As the size of the market research industry shows, there is no shortage of companies happy to peddle their particular version of asking people what they think, and no lack of organizations wanting to pay for the reassurance they feel it provides. As Tim Dewey, who has held senior marketing positions in several blue-chip companies, put it, "People use different stages of research so that if the initiative is unsuccessful they can say, 'Look how thorough I was. I did my due diligence.' In my experience it comes down to the organizational culture; where there's a fear of failure research is used to avoid getting the blame for a project that fails." Add in our demonstrable capacity to collect evidence selectively to support what we would like to believe, and you begin to understand how market research has flourished even when many of the people using it have first-hand experience of it letting them down.

While many of us are happy to mock the more extreme superstitions of others – donning the team shirt at the last possible moment, putting on shoes in a particular order, using the same tennis ball after serving an ace – they reveal a human willingness to stick with what we believe has helped us in the past.[2] As Derren Brown points out in his book *Tricks of the Mind*, we find ways of making our actions appear to have a bearing on events even when they not only have no reasonable basis for doing so, but also with a disregard for the numerous occurrences when, despite applying them, we have not achieved our desired outcome.[3]

So it is with market research. On the occasions when a research report's findings coincide with a positive outcome, it is taken as proof that the process was worthwhile and contributed positively to the course that was taken. Since we're certain that everyone can accurately report what they've done, what they think, and what they will do, any instance when a research-informed outcome is wide of the mark is swiftly dismissed as an aberration or the result of the corruption of an otherwise legitimate process. This capacity to believe that conscious will drives our actions is a fundamental part of the human condition. It is both the reason that asking people questions isn't likely to lead to genuine insights and the reason people are convinced that it will.

The fundamental tenet of market research is that you can ask people questions and that what they tell you in response will be true. And yet, as you will see, this is a largely baseless belief. In fact, it turns out that the opposite is far closer to the truth. When we ask people a question we make it very unlikely that they will tell us the truth; inviting a "discussion" fares no better. The conscious mind finds it almost impossible to resist putting its spin on events. From the moment we do anything it introduces distortions; when the mind considers the future it does so with an idealism that is both optimistic and simultaneously devoid of any objective assessment of the past.

It's not the waste of money or the buck passing that I see as the biggest threat from this particular superstition. At stake is our ability to make good decisions. As someone once said, a mistake is only really a mistake if you don't learn from it. When market research is allowed into the decision-making process, and when that research is as flawed as social psychology and neuroscience are proving it to be, we lose the ability to learn from our mistakes. Research corrupts an organization's learning process by inserting an erroneous fact – what people think – into the equation. Somewhere between an initial idea and a loss-making scheme, research tells us that we "know" something about what our market thinks. As a result, the inclination is to look elsewhere for the scapegoat. With a complex process feeding into a large organization, other potential culprits are always close at hand and all too often research escapes proper scrutiny.

There *is* a way to obtain a deeper understanding of consumers and make better-informed decisions. When the philosopher Mark Rowlands reflected on his years living with a wolf, he concluded that humans had virtually lost the ability to appreciate the present, so wrapped up are we in dwelling on the past and wondering about the future. The problem he sees this causing is that we both want our lives to have meaning and are unable to understand how they can do so. In our quest for significance, we miss the moment of now.[4] When it comes to market research I believe the same situation exists: what drives us into questioning the *why* and *what will be* gets in the way of us fully appreciating the *right now*. It is in the moment of consumer behavior that we have the best opportunity to understand what is taking place. It is in this moment that we can understand how the environment and presence of other people change what we do – factors that expose focus groups as perhaps the single most misguided tool in the researcher's armory.

The market research industry has been slow to embrace the nature of human consciousness. In *The Emotional Brain*, neuroscientist Joseph LeDoux has mapped the way in which the brain functions at different levels and explained how "much of what the brain does during an emotion occurs outside of conscious awareness."[5] As psychologist Cordelia Fine said in the subtitle to her book *A Mind of Its Own*, our brains distort and deceive us all the time.[6] In *Blink* Malcolm Gladwell asks, "What if we stopped scanning the horizon with our binoculars and began instead examining our own decision making and behavior through the most powerful of microscopes?"[7] He theorizes that "we would end up with a different and better world."

This book explains why we need to apply Gladwell's microscope analogy to consumers and how to do it. It outlines why scientific scrutiny should be directed first and foremost at understanding consumers themselves, rather than merely at the process of summarizing their claims. It reveals what drives customer behavior, how anyone can obtain genuine insights into their own customers, and, with the AFECT criteria in Chapter 8, how much weight decision makers should attach to any claimed "consumer insight." AFECT shows why confidence shouldn't only be judged in relation to the number or representative nature of the people involved in a study. The goals of market research are laudable: the better an organization understands its customers, the more likely it is that it will make good decisions and avoid bad ones. It's just that the approach has been misguided.

You will see that what matters is not what consumers say but what they do and why they really do it. General Motors would have been well advised to embrace this notion when it was developing the Signum, a car designed with backseat passengers in mind. GM gave it extra rear legroom, adjustable rear seats, and an optional pack that included a power point, fridge, and various storage compartments for the people sitting in the back. The company launched the car in 2003. However, as *Top Gear* presenter Jeremy Clarkson demonstrated from an hour spent watching cars traveling along a British motorway, only four had back-seat passengers and, despite his best efforts using long-handled gardening implements, it wasn't practical to drive from the luxurious back seats. The car was withdrawn from GM's range in 2008.

The arrival of the internet as a significant channel for consumption should, arguably, have helped many businesses shake off their reliance on asking customers what they think. With such a wealth of real-time behavioral data available and far easier ways to test alternative approaches, there should be no need to ask people what they think they think, and it should be immediately evident when such testimony proves to be inaccurate. However, the overall trend has been for more market research, not less. Many internet retailers can't resist including a pop-up that invites visitors to complete a short survey. More broadly, the ease, speed, and relative low cost of surveys sent out by email have created a new medium for soliciting opinion. It says much about the strength of faith in market research and the ease with which believers overlook its inaccuracies that, rather than having its shortcomings highlighted, it has prospered online.

It is time for fake consumer.ology to be exposed as a wasteful and misleading diversion, and for it to be replaced with insights based on a genuine understanding of how people think and act.

1

UNDERSTANDING THE
UNCONSCIOUS MIND

Why we buy what we do but can't explain it

The story of New Coke has gone down in marketing folklore. In the early 1980s Coca-Cola's main rival, Pepsi, was making significant inroads into Coke's market share. One strand of its attack was with the Pepsi Challenge, in which Pepsi conducted thousands of blind taste tests and publicized the fact that more people liked its product. Despite questioning the results, Coke's own research got the same result: 57% of people asked to taste both products preferred Pepsi.[1] The Coca-Cola Company undertook extensive further research, which led to the creation of a new, sweeter formula for Coke. This recipe did the trick and turned around the taste test results: now Coke was beating Pepsi by around 7 percentage points. At that time, and given the value of the market the two were competing for, the $4 million spent to research and develop the new formula must have seemed like money well spent.[2]

It's well known that the resulting launch of New Coke as a replacement to the original formula was something short of a complete success. It triggered a large public backlash and the company was inundated with complaints. Within just three months the product had been withdrawn from sale and the original formulation was back on the shelves.

Much has been written about why the market research was misleading and most of the arguments put forward have merit. There's a world of difference between sipping a drink and consuming an entire can of it: the initially sweet hit can become overpowering in much the same way that the first chocolate from the box is heavenly, but the tenth consumed in the same sitting can leave you feeling somewhat nauseous. Separating the product from the packaging also removes the brand from the equation, with the implication that marketing Coke is simply a way of reminding people that your brown fizzy drink exists and can be bought wherever you see the distinctive red-and-white logo.

However, amid all the analysis and explanations, no one to my knowledge has reached the ultimate conclusion to be drawn from the New Coke fiasco: it isn't just that Coke's extensive market research on the new recipe was wrong, it is that no such research can be right, other than by chance. Yes, there were technical flaws in the research process, but that doesn't mean that the theorized remedies would have produced a more accurate answer. Giving people a complete branded can to drink or a crate of them to consume over a month at home would probably have produced a different answer, but not necessarily one that would then have been borne out by reality.

Nevertheless, the belief remains: "Of course you can find out what people think by asking them, you just have to ask them the right questions in the right way." The market research industry has gone on unabashed; companies still believe that reassurance can be found in the exchange of corporate question for consumer answer and politicians that public opinion can be gauged from a poll or focus group. No verifiable alternative has emerged for product development, because the crux of the matter is far more challenging to a business world and research industry that rely heavily on the reassurance that market research provides: consumer behavior is a by-product of the unconscious mind, whereas research is inherently a conscious process.

New Coke highlights just how little companies understand about the role of the unconscious mind (little has changed in the intervening decades). Most organizations don't understand consumer behavior or how and why their marketing works (or doesn't work).

The unconscious mind is the real driver of consumer behavior. Understanding consumers is largely a matter of understanding how the unconscious mind operates; the first obstacle to this is recognizing how we frequently react without conscious awareness. As long as we protect the illusion that we ourselves are primarily conscious agents, we pander to the belief that we can ask people what they think and trust what we hear in response. After all, we like to tell ourselves we know why we do what we do, so everyone else must be capable of doing the same, mustn't they?

The problem of the unconscious mind

Most people can identify with that moment of driving a car when they realize that, for some indiscernible amount of time, they have been driving without conscious awareness. The section of journey has been uneventful, they have progressed without incident or harm, but they have no recollection of what has occurred or for how long they have been consciously absent from the driving process. Contrast this experience with the first time you sat in a car and attempted to coordinate the actions of steering, depressing the clutch, balancing the clutch and accelerator, selecting a gear, timing the release of the handbrake, and so on. I can still recall bouncing my driving instructor away from the traffic lights on my third lesson as I struggled to combine raising the clutch and depressing the accelerator simultaneously. An extraordinarily complicated array of actions is learned and assimilated, to the extent that we can do them without conscious thought. And there can be no suggestion that this is an innate skill: cars have only been around for a century or so and evolutionary development can't work quite so swiftly!

I once inadvertently demonstrated the extent to which the delicate actions of driving are controlled unconsciously while sitting in a queue of traffic. Feeling bored at the slow progress of my journey, I decided to let my left foot do the braking instead of my right. My right foot is entirely adept at slowing the car down by pressing a pedal; it knows just how hard to press to bring the car to a stop smoothly. My left foot, even though it was in an unfamiliar place, evidently couldn't change the habit it had developed from depressing the clutch, an action that I came to appreciate requires a much longer, firmer push. The result was an emergency stop. Even though the car couldn't have been traveling at more than ten miles an hour, it was sufficient for the seatbelt-locking mechanism to engage to save me from banging my head on the windscreen, and for the person behind to wonder what the hell was going on!

The unconscious mind isn't solely preoccupied with physical actions. The way in which we acquire language skills as very young children, including complex grammar, occupies an area of the brain that allows us to know that, for example, "we were winning" is right, but "we was winning" is not. We create sentences such as these without conscious reference to the rules of grammar; many people do so in the absence of knowing these rules at all, at least without knowing them at a level where they can express them.

So what is happening in those moments when we don't consciously know what we're doing? How are we making decisions? How accurately can we be expected to self-analyze and report on our behavior?

What would it mean if this phenomenon were not unique to matters of transportation? What if we often do things without being aware that we are doing them? What if that is often the case when we are choosing or consuming products? How useful would it be to ask consumers what they think about a brand, product, or service if the unconscious mind plays a part in their consumption?

We are surrounded by examples of how the unconscious mind and conscious mind behave very differently, examples that show the contributions that each makes to the way we behave. One function of the unconscious mind is its ability to screen out information, enabling us to focus on one area more effectively. A 2 year old who has yet to develop these powers will find a shop far more distracting (as any parent in a hurry will testify).

Similarly, a mother may sleep through a storm but immediately wake if her child coughs (fathers may do this too, but they wouldn't let on if they did). Golfers will play their best shots outside of conscious awareness, and will be unable to recall all the movements their body made in executing a perfect shot, causing frustration when they can't replicate it on every occasion they stand over the ball. We walk or run without any conscious sense of triggering the complex sequence of muscular contractions required.

The more familiar and efficient the process is (or any one part of it is), the more likely it is to be driven by mental processes outside of conscious awareness. How much of an American consumer's soda-buying process is not conscious? The consistent branding of the pack, selected from the same point on the shelf in the store that is visited every day or every week – there's a strong argument to say that the purchase often functions just like that moment of the car journey, passing smoothly without conscious involvement.

Evolution has equipped us with the capacity to make such decisions automatically. There's no need to look at every pack, scrutinize the list of ingredients, and question whether the experience will be positive. In much the same way as eating the distinctive berry from the same bush hasn't killed us or the other people we've seen eating there, we "know" that particular drink is safe from our initial, cautious, and deliberate encounters and now we can simply take one as we pass, directing our attention elsewhere (whether we want the sun lounger that we've just seen is on offer in the next aisle or making sure we don't get eaten by a saber-toothed tiger). In evolutionary terms, it's easy to conceive how those who could effectively automate more mundane tasks at an unconscious level of mental processing would prosper.

Businesses frequently spend large sums of money investigating what customers think about them. Ironically, it's arguable that the greatest success a brand can achieve is to be selected *without* conscious thought: when it has become so synonymous with a person's desires that the unconscious mind has it as the answer before the conscious mind gets involved in considering the question.

But how do you understand what the unconscious mind thinks? The answer, as I will explain, comes in what people do. However, given that asking people what they think is so much more convenient, first I need to persuade you that people really can't accurately account for their actions, thoughts, and feelings in a conscious way.

We don't really know what we know

It's very easy to demonstrate how detached our conscious mind is from our unconscious. If I gave you a £10 note, how confident would you be that what you had in your hand was a £10 note and not something I'd made illegally in my garden shed? My guess is that you would feel very confident you could accurately identify a £10 note, particularly as distinct from something made by a man who has no experience of making bank notes or specialist forgery equipment at his disposal. When you're handed one as change in a shop, I presume that a cursory glance and feel are sufficient to inform you that you have a legitimate note in your hand, and my guess is that you have invariably been right. However, if I asked you to describe a £10 note to someone who had never seen one so that they could create it from scratch, I'm guessing that you wouldn't get very close to reality. Are the "£" and "10" in the same color? Does the word "ten" appear on the note anywhere? If so, how many times? How many digits does the serial number have? Is it printed vertically or horizontally? What pictures are there? How big is the note exactly? Your unconscious mind has the answers, but your conscious mind is evidently preoccupied with other things!

You can repeat this exercise with no end of everyday items. Many people can't say how the numbers on their watch face are represented, despite it being something they visually reference many times each day, and despite them extracting conscious information about the time when they do.

A relative of mine was recently stopped in the main shopping area near his home and asked to take part in a survey on beer. Seated in front of a computer screen, he was asked which brand or brands of beer he bought. Despite the fact that in the supermarket aisle he knows exactly which product he would select, in the absence of the established visual patterns (including the stylized brand name) that would be available to his unconscious mind, he couldn't consciously think of the brand name "Budweiser" in isolation. He told me that instead, he gave the names of the beers he could remember, despite the fact that they weren't the beers he would buy. The next time he saw a Budweiser pack, he remembered what he *should* have said in the research.

We all experience moments when we can't quite grasp something we feel sure we know. This is because our mind doesn't store the information we reference from our memory in an absolute way. In his infamous "known knowns" speech, former US Defense Secretary Donald Rumsfeld forgot to mention that there are things we know that we can't recall at that moment, what he might have called "unknown knowns" if he'd remembered them. Researchers have used fMRI scans to explore this phenomenon. Asking participants to remember unusual word pairings such as "alligator" and "chair" by putting them into a sentence, they tested their recall of individual words from a list containing a mixture of individual words they had been shown and others they had not, while scanning which regions of the brain were active. Only when the second word was provided as a cue did one area, the hippocampus, become involved, at which point participants were able to recall their sentence with much greater detail.[3]

Our unconscious minds have vast amounts of data that we regularly rely on to make decisions, but we have no direct, conscious access to those processes. And that's a problem if a business is expecting customers to respond accurately in research. Asking someone to taste a sample of a product seems an entirely reasonable thing to do, as does asking them what they think of what they've tasted. On the other hand, the normal purchase process involves neither of these elements, but does involve referencing a different set of mental associations to do with factors such as temperature, thirst, previous experiences of the product, and the context in which you find yourself. When taste-test results are considered in this context, any result they produce seems far less compelling.

We don't always know what we're doing

Recently I was asked to investigate why a new television drama program had failed to achieve good ratings. The television network felt that the program itself was of sufficient quality to merit a reasonable audience and couldn't understand why it hadn't performed better. At a conscious level, viewers appeared to be receptive to the program: I spoke to a number of people who were adamant that they liked drama, liked to watch new programs, and were interested in the subject matter of this particular drama. I knew from information I'd collected in advance that these people were watching television when the program was aired, and even that they had selected a program using an electronic program guide that included this one in the listing. Often the alternative program they had selected was not of particular interest to them, or was one they had watched before. The respondents were adamant that if they had had the option to watch the new drama they would have both seen it and selected it;

therefore, they concluded that the program did not exist, and had not been shown on the night in question (despite the fact that it had).

It transpired that these viewers had scanned the television listings in such a way that they hadn't registered the new program at all. When using this type of reflexive mental processing, the unconscious mind can process established program titles very quickly – they are "linked" to a rich tapestry of previous emotions, stories, and experiences – whereas the new title was, in this context, essentially abstract. The unconscious response to abstraction in the midst of all the other association-laden titles available is to ignore it. Faced with between 30 and 200 channels (depending on which type of digital system they own), people have learned to scan the listings guide very quickly. In essence, for efficiency's sake, the unconscious mind has taken over the practice of selecting a program and the apparent conscious desire to watch a new program on a topic of interest is irrelevant.

When an electrical retailer asked me to investigate its ticket design for washing machines, I found more evidence of the gap that can exist between what people would like to believe they will do as consumers and what actually happens. I asked people prior to buying such an appliance how they would make the decision and they provided a rational set of criteria, generally relating to price and one or two specific product attributes (such as spin speed and load capacity). Each person expected the purchase process to be straightforward; after all, they had owned and used a washing machine for years and were comfortable with the product. However, as I watched shoppers in a store it was apparent that a rational purchase decision, even of a major product such as this, was virtually impossible.

There were 40 white boxes that either were washing machines or looked like them from a distance (washer-dryers being virtually indistinguishable from more than a few feet away). Each product had an information label with up to 20 technical specifications for the product, and further information such as product dimensions, accessories, and extended warranty options. Any customer had at least 800 data points to compare. Assuming that they could consolidate their choice by two variables, say spin speed and price, this would still represent 80 data points to weigh up!

Arguably, a logical response to this would be to grab a pen and paper and start writing things down, design a spreadsheet to compare them, or at the very least seek independent advice from someone who might have had the capacity to make such a comparison. However, the very real need for a washing machine and the prior belief that such a purchase *should* have been simple must compete with the unexpected complexity and confusion that the actual task of buying one has introduced. Often this cognitive dissonance isn't manifested as a rational awareness that buying a washing machine is harder than had been anticipated; it arrives as feeling of awkwardness, as though the unconscious mind throws out a generic "error" message.

So what happens? Either the unconscious screens out options at a very general level and defaults to something familiar, or the customer lets someone else (the salesperson) make the decision for them, or they walk away, making up a reason why they haven't got a product they really do need. The resulting rationale for their actions can be extremely tenuous. One woman I interviewed justified her selection by saying: "I decided to get this brand because my mother had one that lasted for years, although I know they don't make these as well as they used to." I had watched her spend several minutes comparing, or at least attempting to compare, machines from several manufacturers at a similar price point and hypothesized that the process had become overwhelming. When I discussed her experience in the context of the confusion that I suspected she'd experienced, she said she had wanted to look at a wider range and make an informed choice, but had been overcome by the number of alternatives.[4]

When I put just two tickets in front of her and asked her which appliance she thought would better suit her requirements, she changed her decision from the Hotpoint she had selected to buy to a Whirlpool model. It confirmed my theory that her chosen purchase had far more to do with the psychological discomfort of making a choice from so many options and far less to do with her rationalized washing machine ideals.

This example highlights another conflict between the conscious and unconscious mind. When you ask them, most people say they want choice; often it will be a conscious consideration when selecting a retail outlet for a purchase – "I'll go to X because they have the biggest range." Choice is a good thing, isn't it? Social psychologists Iyengar and Lepper carried out an experiment that illustrated how, in practice, more choice isn't necessarily beneficial.[5] They evaluated reactions to two tasting tables at a supermarket; on one they laid out 24 different jams and on the other just 6. While more people elected to stop for the wider selection (60% vs 40%), a dramatically higher proportion purchased from the selection of six jams, whereas only 3% did so from the larger choice. Put another way, less than 2% of people will buy from a display of 24 jams, but 12% will if you give them a choice of just six.

This simple but elegant study illustrates the point perfectly: what someone thinks they want, and will say they want because it seems sensible and reasonable, may conflict with what really matters to their unconscious mind when the moment in question arises. At that point it will be the unconscious mind that determines what happens next.

Google made the mistake of asking customers how many results they wanted to see on each page after using its search engine. People responded to the rational question in a rational way – if you're searching for something of course more choice is better. However, when Google tripled the number of results it provided, it found that traffic declined.[6]

The nature of a conscious response says much about a respondent's conscious values and how they would *like* to perceive themselves, but can reveal very little about what really has driven their behavior in the past or what they will do in the future. For example, there are thousands of people each year who resolve not to overeat; they generate a well-intentioned conscious response to the tightness of a favorite pair of jeans, or their doctor's health warning. However, only a small proportion of these people will develop sustained new eating and exercising behaviors. This is not because their conscious intention was insincere, but because the unconscious drive to eat in response to particular physical or emotional stimulus will cut in and trigger consumption irrespective of their conscious intent. In the end, the unconscious drives that we might characterize as habit, emotion, or impulse often exert a much stronger influence over behavior than conscious intent. It's no coincidence that fast-food companies often launch healthy products that customers don't actually buy. In research, McDonald's McLean, KFC's Skinless Fried Chicken, and Pizza Hut's low-cal pizza all appealed to customers, but in restaurants they failed.[7]

Ultimately, the reasons that are consciously hypothesized for consumers' choices – and this is a large part of what makes the New Coke story a valuable lesson for research in general – end up being a reflection of the desire to see ourselves as fundamentally conscious creatures. It's hard to believe that people would buy a drink for any reason other than that they liked the taste, and it's entirely logical to suppose that finding a taste they like better, however one approaches that, is a laudable goal. But the unbridged gap between the conscious and unconscious mind makes the exercise largely futile. Asking people to focus consciously on the difference between two alternative drinks produces a preference (as you'll see in a moment, it can even produce a preference if the products are identical), but the unwitting detachment of the unconscious mind triggers involved in the real-world decision to buy make that conscious evaluation an irrelevance.

All of this raises the question: just how much of what we do as consumers is unconsciously driven? This is where the story becomes fascinating or slightly unnerving, depending on how you look at it, and the case for consumer insights that aren't dependent on people's ability to explain themselves becomes particularly compelling. It's also the point at which elements that can be leveraged to connect with the unconscious mind of the shopper emerge. Traditional marketing theory preoccupies itself with meeting customers' needs, but market research can only identify those needs of which customers are conscious. When my computer breaks I know I *need* a replacement (at least I do if I'm going to finish writing this book). But the vast majority of products are not consumed out of such necessity. Frequently an emotional desire drives people to spend and we're beginning to identify some of the elements that trigger the feeling of "want."

The triggers of desire

Social psychologists are continually exploring the ways in which we are unaware of what really shapes our behavior, and the extent to which it is at odds with our self-perception.

Recent research has shown that smells that are too faint to be consciously detected can influence how we act. Our senses are constantly filtering information and in doing so they process much more than they bother to bring to our (conscious) attention. Dr. Wen Li and colleagues at Northwestern University asked people to sniff bottles containing one of three scents at such low concentrations that most participants were not aware of having smelled anything.[8] They were then shown an image of a face with a neutral expression and asked to evaluate its likability. The researchers found that the type of smell influenced the reaction to the face, but only when the smell had not been consciously noticed. Our unconscious mind is great at collecting data, but it doesn't let our conscious mind in on what it's collected or how important it has deemed it to be, nor how it has influenced what we've gone on to do.

In another study, researchers put one new pair of Nike running shoes in a room with a light floral smell and another identical pair in an unscented room. Afterwards, 84% said they were more likely to buy the pair in the room that smelled of flowers. Yet another study found that pumping a scent into one part of a casino led to people putting 45% more into the slot machines.[8]

The same is true of our visual sense: how people respond can be influenced by things their eyes have seen that they haven't consciously registered.[9] Bargh and Pietromonaco conducted one such study where participants were asked to take part in an exercise on a computer screen, during which half were exposed to words flashed on the screen at a speed too quick for conscious awareness.[10] The words were associated with antagonism (such as "hostile," "insult," and "unkind"). In a subsequent, and ostensibly unrelated, experiment, the same people were asked to make a judgment about someone based on an ambivalent description about him: "A salesman knocked at the door, but Donald refused to let him enter." Those who had seen the flashes of hostile words judged the person to be more hostile and unfriendly than the group who had not seen these words.

There is some evidence that such priming can even override conscious processing. Draine and Greenwald flashed words on a screen and asked people to make a very quick judgment as to whether those words meant something good or bad.[11] They also flashed priming words even more quickly, beneath conscious awareness, that were also good or bad in meaning. When the priming word and overt word were mismatched, the researchers found that people would frequently make a mistake about the meaning of the word they had seen.

While studying the impact of single words is one thing, certain images (particularly relating to female faces) have also been shown to influence how people respond subsequently, so an image on a shop wall, an actress in an advert, a smiling female shop assistant, or a female research interviewer may all change the outcome of the consumer's experience.

The price label on an item can also prime expectations and alter how people actually experience things. Researchers in California found that participants in their research consistently gave higher preference ratings to a wine just because it was priced higher. Having given participants in the research the same wine, but different information about the purchase price, they asked them to rate how much they liked it. Although we might all like to believe that our palate is far too discerning to be led solely by price, we shouldn't be quite so sure. The researchers conducted brain scans during the experiment, which revealed that the area of the brain believed to be responsible for encoding pleasure relating to taste and odor showed increased activity when the participant had been told that the price was higher. Since people believed that the experience would be better (on the basis of the financial context of the wine, in other words its price), the reward centers of the brain encoded it as feeling better.[13]

Other studies have observed consistently different responses from variations in light levels and from differences in temperature. Romantic moments are often associated with the lights being slightly dimmer and a pleasantly warm temperature; is it a coincidence that these same environmental conditions have been shown to make people feel more positive about a neutral stimulus?

Two other studies demonstrate how little we understand about what shapes our own reactions and the potential prize for marketing that connects with the unconscious mind. Diners at a restaurant in Illinois were given a free glass of wine to accompany their meal. In each case the actual wine used was the same (and inexpensive). However, different bottles were used to signal different wine qualities. Where the wine was perceived (purely from the label) as being better, people rated both the wine *and* the food as tasting better, and ate more of their meal. In a second study, people given a wine they believed (from the packaging) was from a superior region rated the wine 85% higher and the food 50% higher.[14] How many of these people, if interviewed two weeks later in their local High Street, would have said: "I enjoyed the meal because the wine looked nice"?

Unfortunately (for consumer research), all these studies are interesting for the very reason that the people taking part *can't* attribute their responses and behavior to the variable being manipulated by the experimenters. What people see, hear, and feel influences their behavior, but they can't account for what has happened or how it has influenced them. However, this inability to understand ourselves doesn't stop us answering questions in research.

Of course, all these unconsciously processed elements exist in every consumer experience. We don't buy products in white-walled, sterile laboratories devoid of smells or visual content. Marketing, in all its forms, is surrounding products with associations. However, as any brand that isn't experiencing soaring sales will testify, marketing is a fairly hit-and-miss affair. This is precisely because it is success at the level beyond conscious awareness that is required, but conscious appraisal that is directing the show. Getting all the elements *around* a product right allows us to *feel* desire, however it may ultimately be expressed and rationalized consciously. Indeed, in most studies conscious awareness of potentially subliminal influences entirely negates their impact. Utilizing the sphere of unconscious influence around your product is one thing, but it only works if you accept that the people it is influencing will never be able tell you directly that it's working.

Learning to ignore the "voice of the customer"

The fact that people can't accurately account for what has influenced their behavior in the experiments mentioned in the previous section doesn't stop them creating reasons of their own that appear, at least superficially, to account for what they've done.

The conscious mind is a powerful tool that, for our own sanity, is highly practiced at wrapping our behavior in a veneer that suits our perception of ourselves. Generally, people perceive their own actions as self-generated, well-intentioned, sensible behavior. The extent to which this is an invention will vary, but since the capacity for it so evidently exists, consumer research must at the very least be mindful of the fact that the independent, well-conceived, and logical responses obtained in research are artificially constructed by respondents, however innocently.

An extreme example of this artificial construction was noted by German psychiatrist Albert Moll.[15] After a hypnotic induction, he instructed a man to take a flowerpot from a window, wrap it in a cloth, put it on a sofa, and bow to it three times. Moll then asked the man why he had done that and was told:

> *You know, when I woke and saw the flowerpot there I thought that as it was rather cold the flowerpot had better be warmed a little, or else the plant would die. So I wrapped it in the cloth, and then I thought that as the sofa was near the fire I would put the flowerpot on it; and I bowed because I was pleased with myself for having such a bright idea.*

The man did not consider his actions foolish and was happy with his self-justification.

A more recent example comes from University of Virginia psychology professor Timothy Wilson, who conducted a study with Richard Nisbett in which they set up a "Consumer Evaluation" of four pairs of tights (panty hose). Respondents were asked to say which they thought was the best quality and to explain why they had chosen the pair that they did.[16] The results showed what the psychologists expected: a statistically significant position effect – A 12%, B 17%, C 30%, D 40%. However, the reasons people gave for their choice referenced an attribute such as sheerness, knit, or elasticity. No one spontaneously mentioned that the position had influenced their preference, despite the fact that all four pairs of tights were identical (a fact that went unnoticed by almost all of the participants). While most people know that you need to design research carefully to remove any order effect when presenting alternatives, the key issue here is that people will invent reasons for a preference in research when none can exist!

In a second study, these researchers highlighted more evidence of the potential for misattribution when investigating the impact of noise on enjoyment of a film.[17] College students were asked to watch a film while someone outside the room intermittently operated a power saw. Partway through the experiment the "worker" was asked overtly to stop making the noise, thereby bringing it to the conscious attention of everyone present. The students rated their enjoyment of the film, as did another group who had watched the same film without the disturbance outside. It would be reasonable to suppose that the group who had watched the film with the noise going on in the background would have enjoyed the film less. Indeed, this is what the researchers anticipated and what those taking part claimed was the case. However, their ratings of enjoyment for the film were no different from those whose experience was unadulterated by the noise.

As Daniel Wegner observes in *The Illusion of Conscious Will*:

> *Much of what we do seems to surface from unconscious causes, and such causation provides a major challenge to our ideal of conscious agency. When life creates all the inevitable situations in which we find ourselves acting without appropriate prior conscious thoughts, we must protect the illusion of conscious will by trying to make sense of our actions.*[18]

Quite how far ahead unconscious processes are is an issue at the forefront of neuroscience, but the technology is starting to provide an insight. Very recently, researchers using sophisticated brain-imaging techniques found that they could accurately predict the "free" choice a person would make up to ten seconds before the person made or was aware of making that conscious choice. Noticing the decision we ourselves have made appears to happen quite a long way down the processing hierarchy and as the result of processes to which we don't have conscious access.[19]

Antonio Damasio, professor of neurology at the University of Iowa, describes a study he conducted with an individual, David, with severe learning and memory defects.[20] David had extensive damage to both temporal lobes, was incapable of learning any new fact, and could not recognize anyone, nor recall any part of their appearance, voice, or things they may have said. To explore whether the brain required a link between consciousness and emotions, Damasio created a situation where David experienced three distinct types of interaction from three different people over several days: one was consistently positive, one neutral, and one unpleasant. Later David was shown sets of photographs, each containing one of the people with whom he'd had the interactions, and asked whom he would go to for help and who was his friend. Despite not being able to remember ever meeting the people or anything about them, David selected in a way that proved he had factored in his experience from the previous day, yet he was able to provide no basis for his selections. This extreme case lends further support to the notion that we don't need our conscious processes to act effectively. As Moll showed, when our conscious faculties are working properly, we're adept at creating a justification that works for us.

Our selective attention is continually screening out a huge amount of information but, as I have explained, that doesn't mean that this information isn't being processed. Quite the opposite: in order to screen it out we must first receive it. Studies such as those by Bargh and Pietromonaco show that, while we are not consciously processing it, our unconscious mind can be changed by what passes through it, leaving us with no realization that such a change has taken place and certainly no ability to report it accurately after the event.

The unconscious mind appears to operate as a first-stage pattern checker, the first, and sometimes only, stage in the processing and reacting chain. However, since people have no direct access to the references it's using, consumer research respondents are unlikely to report accurately its role in their decision making. Consequently, the information provided by research that is responded to at a conscious level has bypassed a critical stage of mental processing that may well prevent the person ever acknowledging its existence. There is little point in asking a television viewer what he thinks of a new program's title, if it contains words that his unconscious mind would pass over and filter out of conscious appraisal at the moment that the selection decision is made in reality.

Another (slightly cruel) way of seeing this unconscious filter at work is with young children who are totally absorbed by a television program. If they don't respond to general requests or questions such as "Where are your socks, Martha?", try asking "Is Dolly Della (one of Martha's favorite toys) going in the bin?" in exactly the same tone of voice. Instantly, the unconscious filter kicks in to flag that there is an imminent risk, and the mesmerizing spell of the television is broken. Similarly, some Coke customers may be drawn toward Pepsi by its claims of taste superiority, but that doesn't mean that shaking your entire customer base from their established behavior is a good idea. When the familiar design of the can has changed to deliver the news that the recipe has altered, the most likely reaction is to focus on what has been lost rather than what might be gained.

Practical examples of these unconscious filtering processes and their impact abound with internet retailers. Their capacity to make small changes and observe their impact using split tests that randomly assign visitors to different versions of a website have found dramatic differences in response, and sales can be achieved with alternations that appear incidental and certainly reflect elements of design that we would never consider influential in shaping our own behavior: changing a headline, shifting the position of a message, or using a different color on a page can transform how people react to what is ostensibly the same message. The US retailer BabyAge.com experimented with different layouts that remained true to the existing look and feel of the brand's website and found that it converted 22% more visitors into customers.[21] People would probably like to think their purchase of a nutritional supplement was decided by what it contained and what would be most effective, but when the makers Sytropin tested an informative medicinal theme against one that focused on how people's lives might be after they'd used the product, it found that 50% more people who arrived at the page went on to make a purchase.[22]

While it could be argued that the analysis of New Coke's failure is too easy in hindsight, my basis for suggesting it stems from people's fundamental psychological makeup. As I will explain in the next chapter, there are certain psychological traits that people consistently exhibit and that are far more likely to determine their actual behavior in response to something new than anything they may tell themselves or a researcher asking them questions.

The truth is that consumer behavior is a reflection of the complex brain processes that drive all human actions. The unconscious mind is "in play" far more significantly than most people are willing to acknowledge. As you will see throughout this book, it shapes what we do, how we do it, and why we do it in the first place. In the next chapter I'll discuss how context dramatically changes what people think and do, and in ways that, were it not for the work of social psychologists and neuroscientists, we might never believe are influencing our behavior.

The unconscious mind has a lot going for it. It has the ability to process vast amounts of data from the five senses, the capacity to react extremely quickly (relative to conscious thought processes), and the means to trigger large numbers of complex actions simultaneously. And it's evident from the way in which we can learn skills like driving a car and acquire language that the unconscious mind certainly has the capacity to learn new things. On the other hand, its role in shaping our behavior isn't perfect. With no access to its processes, the first we're consciously aware is when we find ourselves doing or saying something.

Numerous studies reveal that the unconscious mind works in terms of associations. Imagine a scenario where every time you press a square red button you get an electric shock, whereas pressing a circular blue button plays a favorite song. The unconscious makes an understandable connection between the red button and pain that it will use to protect you in the future. Next time you see a button that looks like the red one that shocked you, how likely are you to press it? The conscious realization that an identical button in a different location might not have the same effect may well be something you draw on to overcome your desire not to press the button, but the desire not to press it will come first and require your conscious intervention if you are to overcome it.

Could this be an example of conscious learning rather than unconscious associations? Tests have shown that we are able to detect patterns and adapt our behavior well in advance of having conscious awareness of the calculations our unconscious has made.[23] In a study where participants were gambling on the outcome of a selection from one of two decks of cards (one of which was loaded against them), they exhibited physiological signs that they had distinguished between the risks of the decks (increased skin conductivity response) well in advance of the point at which they could articulate a hunch about which deck was the better choice. Skin conductivity differed by the time the 10th card was selected, yet it took 50 cards for the hunch to be expressed.

You may well think at this point: "Well, if someone can consciously choose to override the desire not to press the red button, surely what matters is what they consciously think." But in most circumstances, and certainly in most consumer scenarios, people aren't challenging themselves (or being challenged) to act against their instinctive response. Instead, their feelings will be triggered by the unconscious associations they process and, just like Moll's hypnotized subject, they will look for reasons to justify that feeling.

In Thomas Keneally's account of his discovery of the story of Oscar Schindler, which became the basis for his book *Schindler's Ark* and the film *Schindler's List*, he describes a powerful and moving example of the way in which unconscious associations influence what people do. Among the many amusing and tragic accounts he collected during his travels interviewing Jews who had been protected by Schindler, Keneally interviewed one woman who had a very successful and comfortable life in Sydney, Australia. She confessed that she still took a crust of bread in her handbag whenever she left the house to travel anywhere. Despite being healthy and affluent, and although it was more than 30 years since the horrific events that created them, her unconscious associations from the journey she had made to a concentration camp remained. She felt compelled to have something with her to ward off hunger, however short and predictable the trip. When Keneally later recounted this story to a group of Jewish women in New York who had experienced the same traumatic events, several of them opened their bags and showed him the crusts of bread they, too, carried.

We don't need extreme experiences to find evidence of our own behavior being shaped unconsciously. In all the years I've worked for and with manufacturers and retailers, one factor has been of more concern and made more of a difference to sales in any one period than anything else: the weather. The weather determines how much certain businesses will sell: when it's cold people buy more soup, when it's hot more carbonated drinks. When it's a nice day they'd rather do something other than go shopping; when it's cold and raining they cheer themselves up by going somewhere that's brightly lit and where the serotonin triggered by buying something makes them feel a little better.

Unrealistic expectations

I've used what happened with New Coke as a prime example of just how far our conscious illusions about how our own behavior is driven can go in misleading the actions of a company. Coca-Cola's executives made a series of apparently rational judgments and undertook seemingly reasonable evaluative measures to make a major corporate decision. The smokescreen formed by suggestions that methodological issues were behind the failed product launch, rather than the fault lying with the fundamental failure of market research to understand how the consumer mind actually works, has meant that research has continued to flourish. The notion that risk can be mitigated by soliciting consumer opinion is so tempting that millions of pounds continue to be spent pursuing it. And yet it's regularly reported that over 80% of new product launches fail.[24]

Ultimately, however inconvenient it may be when seeking consumer insight, it is unrealistic to expect consumers to know what they think. Just because we can obtain an apparently rational and consistent response from a sample of people doesn't provide any guarantee that such information is accurate.

It would be reasonable to ask: "When are we able consciously to appraise ourselves, our attitudes, or even our preferences?" From the biggest aspects of human life such as the people we love and the house we buy, to the smallest decisions like the chocolate bar we choose or even that we choose to buy one at all, the involvement of consciousness is partial at best:

◆ Much of the information we hold and reference isn't consciously processed.
◆ We don't have conscious access to such information – we can't describe how we know a £10 note is a £10 note.
◆ The more established and routine the behavior, the more likely it is to be dominated by unconscious drivers.
◆ We don't necessarily have or retain knowledge of our actions when they are unconsciously driven.
◆ The absence of that knowledge doesn't stop us from constructing an apparently sensible rationale after the event, which may bear no resemblance to our actual behavior.
◆ What the conscious mind thinks it wants may well be overridden by the agenda of the unconscious mind when the time comes, at which point habit, emotion, and impulse may well determine the behavioral outcome.
◆ The information that the unconscious mind screens and filters and then factors into decisions is not available for the conscious mind to audit or report. As a result we can't accurately identify what has influenced us at any point in time. Ultimately, what we believe (or would like to believe) influences our choices isn't necessarily what really does.

At the very moment that any consumer research works on the presumption that consumers know what they think about a particular subject, in the sense that this is indicative of how they will behave when the moment of consumption arises, it has made a fundamental mistake.

In the last few years, two professors of psychology have examined the role of the conscious and unconscious minds in human behavior and published their studies. Timothy Wilson documents his findings in the book *Strangers to Ourselves* and Daniel Wegner in *The Illusion of Conscious Will*; the titles provide an apposite summation of their conclusions. The evidence of the distance between the conscious and unconscious is all around us should we choose to look for it: from those times we catch ourselves saying something clever and feeling inwardly pleased, to the moment a tone-deaf contestant is told by Simon Cowell that he can't sing but remains convinced he can.

This does not mean that there is no place for consumer research, but there are significant ramifications for what form that research should take and what faith should be placed in research collected through the interrogation of the conscious mind. Ultimately, the imbalance between a conscious appraisal process and the (at least) partially unconscious one of consumption just isn't reconciled by most research methodologies.

Ironically, given that the consumer research that feeds it fails to take it into account, it could be argued that most marketing leverages the unconscious mind, and indeed that it must do so in order to be effective. In many consumer experiences it is either impractical or impossible to compare the array of products on offer. To operate efficiently, consumers rely on their unconscious mind to make decisions. For example, in a supermarket a shopper may purchase 50 or 100 products. To rationally appraise the merits of each one against its competitors would be extremely time consuming. Instead, we rely on clearly delineated (branded) products that have prior values associated with them – ideally those of personal experience, but potentially those placed there from a memorable or distinctive claim. Is it true that Domestos "kills all known germs dead"? How many consumers could ever say? Only those with chemistry labs, presumably. Is a BMW really the "ultimate driving machine"? The chance that it might be means that a certain type of driver may at least consider the brand when making a purchase, and, in the absence of any meaningful and comparable statistic for what a car is like to drive, this promulgated claim becomes a mental substitute for first-hand knowledge or experiential feeling that could otherwise be referenced.

A fundamental issue for research arises out of the nature of consciousness itself. Since people *can* post-rationalize, and indeed since people are convinced that consciousness drives their actions even when it doesn't and that their conscious self-analysis must be accurate, research questions are virtually guaranteed to get answers. They may very well provide reassuringly convenient and consistent answers. They may even offer answers that can be contrasted between groups in a way that gives reassurance that those answers are correct. However, such consistency or apparently meaningful delineation of responses may have absolutely no bearing on their underlying accuracy. When the business that has commissioned the research acts in accordance with it and puts its product or communication or revised brand strategy or new pricing (or whatever else) into the real world, they may well find that they do not get the reaction they anticipated.

While we can acknowledge that there are times when we don't know what or how we've been thinking (driving the car, for example), we can console ourselves with the notion that we know what we *must* have been doing, and by inference thinking, during that time. The problem is that, as I've demonstrated, we often *don't* know what really caused us to behave in the way we did, although our misguided confidence in post-rationalizing makes false accounts in research seem compelling. In social psychology this misattribution is sufficiently well documented to have its own label – the fundamental attribution error – but it's not a term you'll hear in many research debriefs, although you should. All too often the conscious responses garnered in research, be it qualitative or quantitative, are the myths people like to tell themselves.

Is all research pointless? Not necessarily. It's entirely possible that someone talking about a product, brand, or service will say something in the course of research that is revealing of a fundamental consumer truth and that should be factored into decision making. But this is an exercise in selective judgment. This is just as likely, in fact this is far *more* likely, to be the result of what *one* respondent says, rather than the collective or aggregated opinion of a sample in totality. Considered in this light, there are significant implications for the way in which research is approached, the amount you might choose to spend on it, and the weight you should give the "results."

2

READING CONSUMERS

Insights into the Unconscious Mind

Within the tale of New Coke resides the solution to the problem of understanding the consumer mind, at least in part. How do we know that the research didn't work and the decision was fundamentally misguided? Because the product *was* launched and we know what happened. Reality, not abstract conscious evaluation, revealed that New Coke could not be substituted for the original product. Customers complained that they wanted the original product back. When that was reintroduced New Coke's share fell to just 3% of the market, despite its research-claimed taste advantage.

Inevitably there were many factors that influenced consumer reaction and determined New Coke's lack of success: it became fashionable to be critical of the change, the media spread the message of disaffection, and the marketing has since been described as "inexplicably clumsy."[1] However, all these elements (not to mention countless others) have the potential to arise between any abstract research investigation and the real-world moment of purchase.

Of course, a live trial doesn't have to be a national launch. There are degrees of testing, from swapping in some products on one shelf in one store upwards. Yes, the degree of marketing support that it's possible to include or simulate may be limited by the size of the trial – it's not practical to create a television ad campaign to promote a single-store trial and the cost of small production runs will be disproportionately high. However, I would argue that the benefits of capturing true consumer response, especially the unconscious mind's response, significantly outweigh the limitations. If the product doesn't sell well and you still decide to press ahead, at least you have some idea of the scale of the marketing challenge.

When it comes to testing an idea there can be no substitute for live testing: trialing a concept in a real-life situation and observing what happens (from a suitably discreet distance) as a consequence. Tempting as it may be to believe that an idea can be expressed in conceptual form, presented to a number (large or small) of would-be consumers, and its potential evaluated accurately, it's just not possible.

The challenge, therefore, is to develop live trials to test new or alternative ideas. Online retailers are particularly well placed to assess what really happens when they change elements of their selling space or their product mix. They can even create split tests where customers are randomly directed to one of a number of different versions of their website, enabling comparisons to be made when the broadest environmental influences are identical.

I doubt that many customers, if asked, would say they want fewer products to choose from, or that if you took products away they would say that the range left was bigger – but that's exactly what one retailer client of mine discovered. When the visual clutter of a category was reduced people were happy to spend longer in it, found it easier to distinguish the products and the ones that were of potential interest to them, and could appreciate more of the smaller range available.

Another advantage of live testing is that, surprisingly often, something works, but not for the reason that was originally hypothesized. In this situation an idea that might have been rejected by initial consumer research, because the company's rationale for the initiative wasn't well received, can work because of an accidental by-product that wasn't previously considered. Environmental psychologist Paco Underhill recounts a time when he was asked to evaluate a new supermarket display for a soft drinks manufacturer. When he arrived at the store the products had just been left in a huge pile on the floor, rather than stacked as was intended. Underhill asked to leave the products as they were and, through observing customers for the day, found that a far higher proportion of customers noticed the products than was usually the case for the company's merchandising.[2]

In my own work, a client's new store failed to shift its customers' behavior or product awareness, but my observations prompted the marketing director to consider whether a successful design had already inadvertently been created in another store, which had been designed differently because of space limitations. He was right and that store became the model for future refits.

Owners of small businesses learn this way all the time. Author and business consultant Dave Lakhani recounts an experi-ence he had when he owned a computer parts store in the 1990s. Ordinarily, he separated the components into bins so that cus-tomers could easily find what they were looking for. But on one occasion he arrived too late to sort the stock that had arrived and couldn't organize the products before people started shopping. He discovered that people "went crazy," digging through the mixed boxes looking for what they wanted. Since the products weren't priced, he asked people to offer what they thought was fair, and discovered that this was almost always at least 25% more than he would have charged.[3]

When I worked in the marketing department of a restaurant chain, I was given responsibility for the drinks range we stocked. Having looked at the sales data and cost prices one thing stood out: the beer we sold most of cost us 15% more, giving us a correspond-ingly lower profit margin. I proposed substituting the product con-cerned for an alternative that we could buy for a better price; in fact, because the manufacturer was keen to secure distribution we could buy it at a better price than all the other beers we sold. The directors were anxious, though. The beer I was proposing to drop was the most popular brand in the country and they asked me to research the change first with consumers. Despite the fact that I was also responsible for consumer research, I argued that there was absolutely no point in asking consumers. What would we ask?

"Do you want your favored choice of beer not to be available?"

It seemed inevitable that the answer would be "No."

"What would you do if it wasn't?"

"Go elsewhere!"

The research could easily scare the business away from mak-ing what I was sure would be a profitable decision. I could see no reason why anyone would choose our restaurants on the basis of the beer available. I persuaded the company to undertake a trial in one region. When the change was made, total sales remained unchanged while profits increased dramatically as a result of the increased margin we could make on the less expensive product we'd substituted. Shortly afterwards the change was rolled out into every restaurant with no ill effects.

The key challenge with live testing is to avoid the pitfalls of sensitizing consumers to what is being tested and consequently inducing the artificial reactions that follow when people are tacitly encouraged to shift from unconscious to conscious consideration of whatever is being explored. Even when it's impossible not to involve staff in a test, and therefore their sensitization should be expected and may be transferred to customers, this approach is still vastly preferable to asking customers directly what they think. In addition, by setting up a control condition when the status quo is maintained, the sensitization of staff – at least in so far as they are aware that measurement is taking place – can be factored into the trial.

It is important that the scale of a live trial is considered carefully and, in particular, that thought is given to the nature of consumer behavior. The rational notion that people can be made aware of a product that meets a need they have and that, provided it's available at an agreeable price, they will buy it is just not the case most of the time. If you have a product that has relatively isolated customer interactions, for example a food product like a tin of beans sold in a supermarket, it is reasonable to conduct a one-store trial. A large proportion of people shop regularly at one supermarket and confine their unconscious "attention" to tinned beans to the moment they are in that supermarket and actually getting the product. If, on the other hand, your product is consumed in the presence of other people, a drink for example, then seeing the product in several pubs you visit over a period of time and being consumed by other people like you will have a major bearing on whether you try the product or not. Also, once such a product has been purchased on the first occasion, it has more chance of longer-term success if consumers can repeat their purchase experience again easily. If, by virtue of visiting a different outlet, they lapse back into established (unconsciously automatic) purchase behavior of an alternative product, they are far less likely to develop the familiarity and habituation that lead to frequent consumption and subsequent affinity with the new brand.

Finding a way to live test products, services, and marketing communication ideas is the only reliable way of evaluating consumer response (short of a full launch). Granted, it has the potential to be expensive and there may still be reasons why it can't match a full launch; for instance, it's not always technically possible or financially feasible to replicate large advertising campaigns for a small test. However, given the role of the unconscious mind in consumer behavior, the importance of context (environment) and mindset in response, the problems of asking people in research what they think about something and what they will do in the future, and the distortions of introspection or artificial deconstruction, live testing provides the next best thing to going ahead and launching something anyway. Through appropriate observation of what consumers do in response to the test and, when relevant, by comparison with the status quo, it is possible to obtain genuine insight.

The challenge of testing initiatives in this way is considerable, and most companies give little thought to how they might accommodate it because they have a misplaced faith in market research to provide a substitute. When one considers some industries, however, the proof of consumer research's failings is immediately obvious: publishers of books and computer games, companies making television programs, and the film industry release to the market countless products that fail. Wouldn't it be worth testing these with consumers before launching and saving all the time and expense of producing them? Of course it would, but there's a reason publishers don't forward all the manuscripts they receive to research companies for evaluation in focus groups: they know there's no way of predicting what will be successful and what won't.

Through recognizing the limitations of research and the benefits of live testing, companies have the chance to reconsider how they approach the development of initiatives that might otherwise be left to the distinct vagaries of market research. At present, too many organizations align their projects to a research process that can easily reject a good idea or endorse a bad one. Through taking responsibility for what gets developed, and finding other ways of deciding what to take forward, not least the astute observation of existing customer behavior, companies can dramatically increase their chances of success. When failures occur, there is the opportunity to learn from them and, by removing the rogue variable of solicited consumer opinion, establish more accurately what aspects of the business development process have contributed to that failure.

I mentioned that many large corporate functions can be viewed as attempts to model the "natural" practice of entrepreneurs; at present, consumer research has been allowed to creep in as a substitute for entrepreneurial judgment when it has no right to do so. It is the imagination, tenacity, and flexibility of such people that lead to their ability to capitalize on opportunities, not some mystical power to see inside the mind of consumers and deliver something to them that they didn't know they needed. No model of this process will be failure free, just as no entrepreneur gets everything right, but by using a live testing approach organizations can start to learn how to emulate the innovativeness and flexibility that often contribute to entrepreneurs' commercial success.

When the failure to recognize the importance of consumers' unconscious responses leads to a flawed idea being validated by research and implemented, companies can spend a long time looking elsewhere within the complex commercial chain for the reason that sales are not meeting expectations – "We know consumers like it because of the research, we must have done something else wrong." When the barometer of success *is* those sales figures, there is less scope for failing to see the consumer response to your activity accurately.

Live testing requires people to make real choices that have real and measurable consequences: the risk and opportunity cost of selecting a new product over an existing one; the requisite shift out of engrained patterns of behavior to notice something different; breaking through the unconscious filtering of visually busy retail environments and the distractions of shopping in real life.

As I mentioned in the previous chapter, there are common psychological traits that, despite often contradicting what people claim, typically influence their behavior. These are the unconscious traits that any marketing must be mindful of if it is to be successful. Had Coca-Cola appreciated these it might well not have ended up being described as the architect of "the marketing blunder of the century."[4]

Never mind the upside – loss aversion

The idea of getting something new is, for most people, exciting and appealing. A casual glance at the pace of progress in the developed world and the rate at which people assimilate new products is a powerful illustration of our collective thirst for innovation. However, what appears to be a taste for novelty, even to the extent that we believe it's something we consciously desire, masks the fact that our first instinct tends to be much more cautious. The thorny problem of a discrepancy between our conscious view of ourselves and the role our unconscious takes in protecting us can all too easily prevent us from selecting something new or different.

This propensity to be risk averse can be challenging to accept. After all, you have all the positive mental associations from new things that you have bought or, even better, been given: the ceremony of unwrapping boxes, the anticipation of the first experience, the thrill of the first time you use whatever it is. But these belie the reality that, on a daily basis, you frequently make an unconscious decision *not* to do something new: to put your shoes on in the same order, to buy the same newspaper every day, to watch an episode of a television series even though you've seen it several times before.

One experiment conducted by Kahneman and Tversky in 1984 and recounted by Kevin Hogan in *The Science of Influence* compares people's reactions to risk by asking them to make a quick gamble from the following pairs of options:[5]

Pair One
Alternative A: A sure gain of $240
Alternative B: A 25% chance to gain $1,000, and a 75% chance to lose
          nothing

Pair Two
Alternative C: A sure loss of $750
Alternative D: A 75% chance to lose $1,000, and a 25% chance to lose
          nothing

The researchers found that 73% of people chose the AD combination. Only 3% chose BC, even though it is a slightly better choice.
While people might like the idea that they are open to new ideas
and willing to take a chance on something, there is no personal
risk in telling a market researcher that you would buy the product
being shown to you in the focus group. When it comes down to
a real purchase decision, however, the unconscious mind's desire
to avoid risks can often make the choice of something new feel far
less appealing.

It's easy to illustrate this type of loss aversion with children
in a different way. Ask them which toys they like and you will get
a list. Then tell them you are going to get rid of several that they
haven't mentioned, are way too young for them, and they no
longer play with, and they will forcefully state that they want to
keep them.

For some reason, presumably of evolutionary benefit, people
feel loss far more powerfully than they feel gain. I sometimes
demonstrate this during presentations to clients by asking someone
for a £10 note. I then give this to another person in the room before
carrying on as if nothing has happened. It's revealing to watch how
difficult it is for the person who lost the money to think about anything else, whereas the person who receives it, while being surprised and grateful, doesn't dwell on the event for anywhere near
as long. You'll almost certainly have experienced this phenomenon
yourself when you realize you've lost something. The desire to find
it can become all-consuming, even if it's a relatively trivial item,
and yet once it's found the joy of discovery is quickly forgotten

and the thing concerned slips back into the humdrum place it occupied in your life before it vanished.

It is intriguing to speculate about why we should be so sensitive to potential loss. One theory is that the unconscious mind is preoccupied with safety, checking the environment rapidly and evaluating what is a potential threat, conducting a first pass of the data to protect us from potential dangers. So when the unconscious recognizes something distinctive and connects it to a benign or pleasant experience in the past (perhaps a glossy ad next to an article about your favorite actor), it can allow us to feel "good" about that option.

The evaluation of advertising usually involves asking respondents what brands they can recall (top-of-mind awareness), conscious spontaneous recall of advertising for a product type or brand, and prompted recall using the advert (or sometimes stills from it); all conscious measures. But what about what the unconscious mind has seen? Research has shown that print adverts processed outside of conscious awareness shift attitudes just as much as those processed consciously. In one study, 80 subjects were exposed to adverts either deliberately (they were asked to look at them) or incidentally (they were asked to assess the layout of the magazine page opposite). Afterwards, the group were asked to rate 50 adverts and say whether they had seen them earlier. Just 11% of those who had seen them incidentally recalled the ads that had been shown, but their ratings of them as more memorable, appealing, eye-catching, and distinctive were just as positively biased over the adverts not shown as those who had been exposed to them deliberately.[6] It appears that the unconscious mind recognizes what it has seen before and, because it is familiar, can process it more fluently, which creates the feeling of liking something more – unconscious familiarity breeds affection! So even where people can't recall seeing an advert for a product, it can "feel" like a better idea to purchase it because it is unconsciously familiar.

One of the ways in which brands themselves work is through risk aversion. Over time, through experience, familiarity, the suggestion of advertising, or the context of positioning, we take reassurance from the name on the pack. It implies a set of standards and qualities for the product that reassure when the factual information that might ideally be referenced is either too difficult or too time consuming to consult. For example, I believe that if I buy a Sony television it will be well made and last a long time, because these are values I associate with the brand. In reality, I don't know if the television I am buying has been made in the same factory, by the same people, with the same quality of components, and with the same quality testing that I assign to the brand. I could probably find out which country it's made in, but that wouldn't tell me very much. I might be able to find an independent review, but that wouldn't be based on a sufficiently large sample of products over a representative lifespan for the product to tell me about the quality; more likely it would have involved one person looking at the television and rating the picture, sound, and, perhaps, apparent quality of the finish. In choosing the Sony brand I feel as though I'm taking less of a risk than buying a brand with which I have fewer or lesser associations.

The extent to which people will go to minimize the risk of feeling bad in the future is considerable. In the project I undertook watching people buying washing machines, I saw one woman wander around the display of appliances for 30 seconds without actually looking at any appliance in a way that suggested she was seriously considering it. Eventually, she stopped by a particular appliance and waited for a salesperson to come over to her. While pretending to be testing the robustness of the hinge on a tumble dryer, I listened in to the conversation that took place. The woman declined the offer of help and advice, stating that she wanted the washing machine in front of her. When the salesperson asked if she had purchased the brand before, she said that her last three machines had been made by the same company; she also expressed the hope that this one wouldn't damage her clothes like the previous two had. Logically, rationally, and (above all) consciously, her choice made little sense. However, viewed as a response to the confusing variety of products on offer, and a fear that a brand of which she had no empirical experience might be worse, the "devil you know" policy makes a sort of sense.

Another way of identifying situations where shoppers are preoccupied by risk is through the questions they ask. A friend of mine owns a guitar shop and recounted the following questions from a customer enquiring about a guitar he was selling at a remarkably good price as the result of a bulk order. The first was: "How many have you got left?" In other words: "Can you reassure me that lots of other people have thought this was worth buying?" My friend advised him that he had just six of the original 100 guitars remaining. "How many do you usually sell on a Saturday?" In other words: "Can you offset my anxiety about spending my money on this guitar by telling me that if I don't I will miss the opportunity and feel worse because of that?" He was informed that the most they had ever sold on one day was six guitars. Finally, the potential customer enquired: "What else do you have for the same money?" In other words: "What might I regret not having bought if I buy this one?" My friend told him that they had several other choices at the same price, but that none of these guitars matched the value, nor had obtained the enthusiastic reviews from guitar magazines that this one had. At no point had the customer made any attempt to establish if the guitar concerned might suit his "needs" better than others; he had never said what style of music he played, which other guitars he liked or had owned, or what amplifier he planned to pair it with. He hadn't asked about the voicing of the pickups, the quality of finish, or how the instrument would be set up (how well it would play). Instead, he revealed that the substantial discount, while having attracted him, was still insufficient to convert him into a buyer.

Being mindful that people are primarily focused on not making a bad choice – in other words making a safe choice, rather than necessarily making the best choice – can provide a powerful insight into why they do what they do, and the lengths to which it may be necessary to go if you are to encourage them to do something different. Unless the environment is such that they are already in a risk-taking mindset (for example at a theme park or perhaps in a night club), or they are making an extremely deliberate and conscious decision, they will require a significant level of persuasion to break with what feels unconsciously safe.

Why do new products often start out with a trial price? Because most marketers realize that a financial discount can not only help get the product noticed on the shelf, but also offset the unconscious risk associated with deviating from the usual choice. While there has been some debate whether what drives this is a fear of risk (loss aversion) or a preference for the status quo over change, the effective result remains the same: people are often very resistant to trying or doing something new, however logically compelling that alternative is.

The conscious mind is far more receptive to new concepts than is the unconscious. New things arouse our curiosity. Knowing which type of thinking is more involved at each stage of a consumer decision is crucial to understanding the likely accuracy of any research methodology. Telling customers that New Coke tasted better wasn't sufficient to overcome their reaction to what they were losing when "old" Coke was withdrawn. As Mark Pendergrast points out, this is perhaps even less surprising when one considers that Coca-Cola had been telling its customers that "old" Coke was "it" and "the real thing" for years! The original product and packaging had all the established associations, all the comfort, familiarity, and safety for the unconscious mind, with those positive emotive associations planted by Coke's likable advertising and sponsorship. Picking up New Coke was like picking a berry from a new bush; the unconscious had every reason to be anxious and look for reasons not to drink it.

A study using brain imaging conducted in 2003 found that the results of the original Pepsi Challenge were more than reversed when participants were shown the packaging of the product they were drinking. When subjects were shown the familiar design of a Coke can before they tasted the product, a different area of the brain became involved and the results changed: significantly more preferred Coke when they'd seen the can design than both Pepsi and an unlabeled sample, even though it too contained Coke.[7]

One classic driver of consumer behavior leverages the unconscious mind's aversion to loss to influence purchase: perceived scarcity. As I learned to my cost during a "traditional Greek dancing" excursion on holiday one year, there's nothing like perceived scarcity to induce a different consumer response. When the unfounded rumor went round the table that the wine was running out, I acted quickly to ensure I got value for money (in my defense, I was a student at the time). The resulting hangover meant that one of seven precious days on a Greek island was wasted and I developed an aversion to retsina that I retain to this day.

Most salespeople know that if they can convince someone that an opportunity to buy a product, or better still the product itself, won't be available later, they can persuade them to part with their money.[8] When a person's fear that they will miss out offsets their perceived risk in making the purchase, they have a powerful motivation to act. How much more quickly do you press the "buy" button when a website tells you it only has one of the product that you're interested in? When the fear of missing out overpowers the fear of making a bad choice, people will buy.

When New Coke was launched and the previous version withdrawn, "old" Coke's perceived value was massively enhanced by its (very real) scarcity. There were stories of people buying up whatever stock they could find and stores selling what stock they had for three times its usual price.[9]

Easy usually wins – mental fluency

I mentioned previously how frequently repeated conscious actions create unconsciously driven behavior. It's worth noting just how much of most people's daily lives function at this level; it is, after all, a highly efficient way of going about life. Studies show that thinking uses glucose, so the more thought any activity requires the more tired we will become.[10]

The extent to which our unconscious mind likes the path of least resistance is both intriguing and slightly disconcerting! Studies have found that stocks and shares with easily pronounceable names are preferred and selected over those with less familiar strings of letters, and that handwriting clarity and font choice also affect how people respond to something.[11] It would seem that our response to words and the style in which they are written is influenced by the associations and filters we unconsciously map onto them. We unconsciously like what's easiest and most familiar; in other words, what our brains can process most fluently. But of course, as is the way with the unconscious, we don't know we're doing this and that it is shaping our judgments. "Oh no," we tell ourselves, "we're making conscious, balanced, desperately sensible decisions." There is evidence that this bias toward fluency starts at a very early age: a study looking at the spelling ability of children aged 5 and 6 found that children's names influence the way in which they approach the spelling of other words.[12]

When the US firm Extra Space Storage tested alternative versions of its website, it found that making a picture of its storage facility larger and adding a more prominent map of directions increased the proportion of people who arrived at the site and went on to make a booking by 10%. A combination of what people presumably found a reassuring image and making it easy to find made an appreciable difference to the business.[13]

Making a conscious decision to buy something new is, quite literally, an effort. It's one thing to be mentally geared up for the process of answering some questions, it's quite another to expect customers to feel good about not being able to go with the flow through the supermarket's beverage aisle and suddenly to invest unexpected energy in a purchase evaluation.

The crowd matters – social proof

Another factor that can help explain why people do things, which again runs counter to our preferred view of ourselves as independent-thinking entities, is our striking propensity for copying what other people do. This capacity has become a topic of great philosophical and psychological interest in recent years under the topic of memes, cultural elements that are passed on by imitation. It has even been argued convincingly that our ability to imitate is what distinguishes humans from other creatures.[14]

When people see others doing something, at the very least they tend to form a view about it, and in many cases will go ahead and copy it. This trait is capitalized on by people who set up temporary market stalls or rent retail space for a short period. They know that if they get a few "friends" to stand around them as they start to sell, other people will stop too. Once there's a crowd present a few of those friends start getting excited and rush to buy the "amazing" deals on offer; other people start to follow their lead.

While most of us would like to tell ourselves that we wouldn't be taken in by the temporary shop scam, we are unconsciously influenced in many other ways by what other people are doing. The language we use, even our inflexion when saying the words, the fact that we acquire language at all and that we talk so much, all reflect our love of copying and having ourselves (and our ideas) copied.

In one experiment, researchers put people into a room into which they started to blow smoke. For the most part people on their own sensibly went to report it, but when others were planted who didn't react to the apparent emergency, more often than not the ones who weren't aware that the smoke wasn't the sign of something serious didn't either. In another study, when someone was heard to fall off a ladder nearby, 70% of individuals went to help, but when a couple of people were added to the room who had been told to act unconcerned by the noise outside, just 7% felt the need to go the person's aid.[15]

An intriguing aspect of our willingness to follow the flock is that we don't actually need to see the flock ourselves: it's enough for someone to tell us what the flock is doing. Psychologists looking at how people react to signs requesting that hotel guests use their towels for more than one day found that far more people did so when the message explained that most of the people who'd used the room before them had reused their towels.[16] Another study looking specifically at consumer attitudes found that consumers who had been asked to evaluate products individually, and were then told that their peers had evaluated the same products negatively, were heavily influenced by what they heard.[17]

It's no surprise, then, that consumer fads are so commonplace. Products come along and seem almost essential, so compelling is our desire to buy them, and yet within a matter of months the excitement passes. Inevitably another fad soon follows, revealing both the extent to which we are influenced by what goes on around us and our inability to distinguish what's truly useful from what seems like a good idea because everyone else is doing it.

For a period in the 1990s people in the UK, particularly teenagers, were hugely excited about being "Tangoed." The phrase "you've been Tangoed" was quickly assimilated as a euphemism for shocking someone and, most importantly, was passed around from person to person. Nowadays many people wouldn't be able to tell you if the brand still exists (it does). One of the most important elements in determining the success of a book, film, or television program is the extent to which its publicity gets talked about; this is arguably a far better indicator of success than the quality (however that may be judged) of the entity itself.

When it comes to understanding consumer behavior, despite what most of us would like to tell ourselves, at an unconscious level we aren't individual pioneers, we're sheep.

What is first matters most – priming

It's almost impossible to overestimate the importance of what people encounter first for what they go on to think. Much as we may all like to pretend that we're objective, well-balanced, and rational judges of what we encounter, research shows that we're primed by our first experiences and, from there, go about seeking evidence that will fit with what we've decided is right.

As an example of how people are influenced by what they see or hear first, consider the following two calculations:

$$1 \times 2 \times 3 \times 4 \times 5 \times 6 \times 7 \times 8 = ?$$
$$8 \times 7 \times 6 \times 5 \times 4 \times 3 \times 2 \times 1 = ?$$

The average guess for the first calculation is 512, for the second 2,250, more than four times higher. Of course, the actual answer is exactly the same (and, for what it's worth, considerably higher than people guess: 40,320), but what happens is people attach far greater significance to the first few numbers and estimate an answer accordingly.[18]

The same is true with words. People can be asked to consider two people and quickly decide who they think they would like more:

John is intelligent, industrious, impulsive, critical, stubborn, and jealous.
Mark is jealous, stubborn, critical, impulsive, industrious, and intelligent.

It shouldn't make a difference, since the descriptions contain exactly the same words, and yet most people unconsciously attach more weight to the words they hear first and say they prefer John to Mark.[19]

Priming and social proof can work together to exert a powerful unconscious influence on the way people behave. Another example of our being far less autonomous than we would like to think stems from our susceptibility to other people's statements. In one study, participants were asked to play a game in which mutually beneficial outcomes were much more likely if they were trusting and trustworthy. They could either keep a sum of money or give some to the (fictitious) other person; if they chose to give the money away it would be trebled and the recipient would have the option to give some back. Two aspects made the game interesting: first, the person with the money was given a character profile of the recipient that indicated their moral character, but they were warned that that person's responses in the game might not reflect the descriptions they'd just been given, and in fact people painted as morally "good," "bad," or "neutral" would all share 50% of the time. The second aspect was that the participant's brain activity was being mapped during the exercise. It transpired that, despite realizing that all three fictitious partners were sharing at about the same rate, people continued to favor the partners they had been told were good. What the imaging showed was that the area of the brain usually associated with experience was only activated for the partner who had been depicted as neutral. Where people had been told something was good or bad, they no longer processed the evidence in the same way and consequently didn't adapt their choice on the basis of what they were experiencing. The primed third-party information was given higher priority than the first-hand experience.[20]

In perhaps the most extreme experimental example of how being primed with information can be persuasive, people who took part in a study on social sensitivity in which they were asked to distinguish between genuine and fake suicide notes were arbitrarily told that they were either good or bad. Even after being informed later that the results were fictitious, people went on to rate their expected performance in a future test of their social sensitivity on the basis of the erroneous feedback they'd been given first of all.[21]

If we think back to New Coke, it was one thing being introduced to the new formula via a blind test, quite another being introduced to it by the wave of negative publicity that ensued within a few days of its launch. The media were captivated and within days it is claimed that 96% of Americans knew about the flavor change. Coca-Cola executives initially assumed that they were getting great free publicity, but it came at a price: consumers were being primed with the social proof that this new drink wasn't appealing to Coke drinkers.[22]

Understanding the nature of priming is vital to understanding consumer behavior. First experiences, first brand messages, first impressions, first sensory experiences, and the first things people say about a product are hugely influential. If consumers pick up on a message they will unconsciously seek evidence to support it. The conscious notion that reason or balanced judgment might win through simply does not apply.

Crucially, potential primes are all around. As you will see later on, inadvertent priming is an inevitable consequence of almost every market research process.

Summarizing the lessons from New Coke

As I said before, the reason to reflect on the development and launch of New Coke doesn't lie in the blunders made by one company, albeit one of the world's biggest brands. Rather, Coca-Cola's use of market research relied on a rational model of consumer thinking that is totally at odds with actual behavior. It's a mistake worth understanding, because it's one that companies continue to make and through which they waste large sums of money, pursue flawed initiatives, and strangle what could be perfectly good ideas.

It's easy for any initiative to be appraised consciously in one light and responded to quite differently when the unconscious is in full flow. If some accounts are to be believed, the New Coke launch can be summarized as follows: Pepsi tells customers that, after masses of blind taste tests, people think its product tastes better than Coke and, even though pretty much everyone has already tasted both, customers start to drift away from Coke. Coca-Cola changes the formulation of its product until it finds one that beats Pepsi in taste tests and replaces its old recipe with the new one, telling the world that it's giving them a new coke that tastes much better (a "fact" it confirmed at great expense). Initially people are taken in (one source claims that Coke's sales grew initially by 8% year on year, although this could have been weather related and I haven't seen a claim that its market share went up over this time), then a public and media backlash emerges because people want the original product back. Within three months the original Coke is relaunched and sales of New Coke fall away dramatically. At the end of the whole process, Coca-Cola emerges as the dominant cola brand once more.

Along this journey we discover that taste isn't taste when it's branded taste, a sip isn't the same as a can, people prefer to buy without thinking, hate losing something more than they like getting something new, are hugely influenced (primed) by what they first encounter, and, in spite of anything else, will follow the crowd if they get the chance. What market research was going to predict that?

Of course, among the four factors that preoccupy the unconscious mind are the reasons that research has flourished. First and foremost, research is perceived as a means of reducing the inherent risk in decision making. It has become so established that anyone starting a job in a large organization over the last 30 years will have found the principle and mechanisms for research easily accessible; it's the default thing to do. Just as with managed investment funds, the majority of whom underperform the market average, successes are trumpeted and failings, for the most part, quietly discarded.

The impression, or social proof, appears to suggest that everybody is doing it and it's working well; indeed, it would take a brave person to discard such an apparently benevolent tool. The heady cocktail for the unconscious mind is complete if the first encounter is felt to have been a success.

While our awareness of the nature of the unconscious mind and the way in which it shapes behavior is relatively recent, social psychologists and neuroscientists are helping us to understand processes that are far from new; it's likely that they have been around for thousands of years. Companies have much to gain from recognizing the considerable limitations of market research and the role and nature of the unconscious mind in consumer behavior. Live testing isn't perfect, but it does tacitly acknowledge the place of the unconscious mind.

However, what about those situations when an organization wants to understand its existing customers better? Understanding the relationship between the way consumers think and the context in which they consume is a good place to start.

3

THE CONSUMER IN CONTEXT

Environmental influences

If you want to know why someone does or doesn't buy, you have to understand how the environment shapes behavior. Divorcing the quest for understanding from the context in which it takes place is a recipe for leading yourself astray. To maximize sales or the impact of communication, the environment has to be right.

Over the past 20 years numerous studies have revealed how our behavior is influenced by elements of the retail environment that should, logically, have no bearing on what we choose to do. While it may not be a revelation to learn that music and lighting can affect our mood and, as a result, our behavior, the extent to which both can cause people to spend more *is* surprising, as well as further evidence that we're not equipped to be aware of what shapes our own behavior.

In general, consumer research is conducted in a place that is convenient to the researcher.[1] Indeed, research tends to come labeled according to where the data is obtained: in-street interviews, online surveys, in-home, hall tests, viewed (viewing facility) groups, and so on. Implicitly, the message is clear: it doesn't make any difference where you ask questions, you'll get the same response. As I will discuss in the next chapter, there is much to be learned from watching what people buy and how they buy it, but first I should explain why the environment matters so much, how it can change what people do, and what a dramatic difference it can make to sales.

Charles Areni, who specializes in studying the environmental psychology of commercial space, set up a test in a shop that sold wine, playing either top 40 or classical music. He found that people spent more than three times as much on a bottle of wine when classical music was playing compared to when pop music was selected.[2] Of course, all the people involved assumed that they were buying the wine they wanted to buy and would be able to provide apparently rational justifications for doing so, but they didn't know that the quiet background music was the only variable being altered. Recently, a wine industry provocateur has said he believes the taste of wine is influenced by what music is playing; a bizarre theory perhaps, but one that makes sense when one considers the impact of unconscious mental associations and potential for misattribution that psychological studies repeatedly encounter.[3]

For instance, researchers have found that the type of music played can dramatically alter the amount of time people stay in a store and how quickly they move, and can change their perception of how long they're kept waiting or how crowded the shopping area is.[4] Not surprisingly, these influences on behavior and perception can lead to greater spending; a comparison of slow and fast music in a supermarket found that the former led to 39% higher sales.[5] Again, no one would suggest that these people walked out thinking: "I definitely spent more because all the music was less than 60 beats per minute."

In the US, psychologists experimented with changing the lighting in two retail displays, one featuring tools in a hardware store and another with belts in a western apparel and feed store. They installed additional 500-watt lighting in the ceiling, which they could control independently from the main lighting in the room. Through videoing the shops' customers they recorded the amount of time people spent at the display, the number of items they touched, and the number they picked up. They found that consumers who engaged with the displays touched more of the items and spent significantly longer there when the additional lighting was turned on.[6]

It is well documented that light levels have an effect on brain chemistry: light regulates the body clock and is associated with the release of serotonin, which plays an important role in the regulation of mood, anger, and aggression. However, only people who've been diagnosed with a condition such as Seasonal Anxiety

Disorder might be expected to recognize that they'd feel better if they got more light. It is entirely reasonable to suppose that if the light in the research environment is significantly different from consumer reality, people may feel and react differently.

Beyond the way in which changes in lighting and music cause people to behave differently, more subtle variables such as the proportions of the room have been shown to change how people think; the very nature of their thought processes appears to alter. Two marketing professors created four rooms that were identical except for the height of the ceiling, which they set at either 8 or 10 feet. By giving participants different tasks that required different types of mental processing and analyzing the results, they discovered that people in rooms with higher ceilings performed better at tasks requiring relational processing (to do with identifying and evaluating the connections between different sports), whereas when the ceiling was lower participants performed better at item-specific tasks. They also found statistically significant differences in how two products were evaluated.[7] Of course, no one taking part was told that ceiling height was the focus of the study. Just like the research on subliminal smells and images revealed in the previous chapter, these environmental influences take place at an unconscious level and, through some twist of evolutionary fate, our conscious minds are oblivious to what's really driving the thoughts, feelings, and behavior that result from them.

The human environment

Another influential aspect of context that consumer research routinely fails to consider is who else is present during an influential phase of the consumer experience. Anyone who has ever been in a shop with a young child will know that the retail experience can be dominated to a far greater extent by the child's actions than by any other environmental variable. A 2 year old will want to stop and touch a huge proportion of the products and displays. Depending on the circumstances this could have a number of effects on the adult concerned: noticing something that would

otherwise have been screened out; reduced sensitivity to unconscious environmental influences; or the desire to abandon the consumer experience altogether!

In one study, the time spent shopping at a DIY store was
compared for different combinations of consumers.[8] Women shopping with a female companion were observed to spend on average
more than 75% longer in the store than a woman and a man shopping together. It is relatively easy to analyze one's own experiences
and speculate on why this might be the case. Irrespective of the
reasons, the fact remains that people's thoughts and feelings as evidenced by their behavior must be markedly different in these contrasting circumstances.

As consciously capable, self-rationalizing beings, we prefer to
believe that we are the sole masters of our choices and our destiny,
however much an objective assessment of our lives may contradict
this. How many of us recognize that we have been influenced by
an advert or the actions of a salesperson? Even where we can
grudgingly acknowledge their presence, most of us prefer to believe
that a salesperson's involvement was only one (very marginal) factor in our decision, rather than the critical point of influence that
determined the outcome of our experience. Of course, any retailer
that monitors sales on an individual staff basis will be able to point
to one person who generates considerably more sales than another,
over the same period of time in the same retail outlet. Their efficacy *could* conceivably be attributable to work rate, but when you
spend a reasonable amount of time watching different salespeople
in action you soon see that some have skills in sizing up customers,
developing a rapport with them, and then tailoring their sales
approach as required. Ultimately, the outcome of a consumption
occasion can be entirely determined by the human interaction that
takes place with the salesperson.

It is fascinating to observe how good salespeople get customers to tell them what they will be influenced by, and then
leverage that dimension later. I'm not suggesting that this is duplicitous in nature; anyone whose job it is to make sales and who has
the interpersonal flexibility to try different approaches will unconsciously assimilate an understanding of what works and what

doesn't. Sometimes it's as simple as asking if the customer has a particular brand in mind. If the customer volunteers a brand name that the store stocks, the salesperson can eulogize about that brand and have a very good chance of making the sale. The alternative, suggesting that a brand the customer proposes is somehow inferior to another, carries a significant risk of undermining the customer's confidence and causing them to go away "to think about it."

Of course, a combination of poor training and an absence of interpersonal flexibility can create a very different effect. I vividly recall going to look at a car at a dealership several years ago and the salesman repeatedly asking me what was stopping me buying the car I'd taken for a test drive. My issue was a fundamental one – the car wasn't quick enough – but rather than acknowledge this and offer an alternative car, he pursued a bad script and asked: "If we could overcome that would you buy it?" I could see no practical way of changing the car's performance and he didn't suggest one, so the conversation quickly became mystifyingly abstract. I didn't buy the car, or a faster one, from that salesman. I don't know if he is still selling cars, I'm not sure if he ever sold a car come to think of it, but I suspect that there is a salesperson somewhere who would have approached things differently and persuaded me at least to stay in touch with the dealership.

The impact of the presence of other people is demonstrably significant even when, logically, it should make no difference. As you will see throughout the book, and particularly in Chapter 5, there are numerous reasons to question the validity of responses obtained to questions. However, one aspect is the way people's answers to questions change depending on the way they are asked. Online surveys are becoming hugely popular because of their relatively low cost and high speed, but people give different answers to certain questions when they are sitting in front of a computer screen alone from those they express when someone is there to ask the question. In one study, the answers to questions such as "How do you manage on your income?" varied between 29.9% and 47.7% saying they were "comfortable," depending on whether the question was answered in the presence of someone else or not.[9] Another comparison, conducted by a large opinion polling

company, found that 73% of people interviewed by telephone who
thought prison sentences should be served in full disapproved of
muggers being spared a term in prison. The same poll conducted
online at the same time found that only 52% fell into the same category. Despite the pollsters ensuring that the two samples were
weighted to reflect the demographics of the UK population as a
whole, they obtained statistically significant differences to 22 out of
28 questions![10]

The market research industry's reaction to such anomalies is
to scrutinize the approaches used and ask: "Which method is more
accurate?" The answer to this inherently biased question is "neither": what we think is a by-product of where we are, what and
who we're surrounded by, and how we happen to be thinking at
that moment in time. It may well be that, in the presence of someone whose job it is to stand in a street on a cold day and plead
with people to come and answer a few questions, more people
consider themselves well off. Conversely, when they are sitting in
front of their computer answering tedious questions in the hope of
winning £5,000 in a sweepstake for participants, part of them asks:
"How has my life come to this?" Of course, if you've just been
stopped in the street by someone collecting for starving children in
Africa, or watched the people of Haiti fighting for their lives, your
answer will be different again. In trying to quantify such nebulous
concepts in any way, market research is really missing the point.

Almost everything is relative

Another aspect of the consumer environment consists in the products and product communication that surround any given item.
Research has shown that the result of advertising is influenced by
the context in which it is placed. In tests where the context of the
magazine or program was similar to the subject of the ad, it
resulted in better understanding and greater likability of the advert.
A good feeling about the context is misattributed to the ad itself.[11]

Where participants who knew a lot about cars were asked to
evaluate an advert for a Honda, they rated it more favorably when

it was surrounded by ads for prestigious brands like Armani and Rolex, than when it was in the context of less premium brands like Timex and Old Navy.[12] When Simonson and Yoon compared how people evaluated the attractiveness of a series of products, including lawn mowers, food processors, and cars, they found that the strength of preference for a product was influenced by the context of choices presented at the time. For example, when a pen was selected from a set where it was significantly better than another, participants would pay more for it and think it wrote better than when the same pen was selected from a more balanced set of options.[13] With the vast sums spent on advertising, a relatively small investment replicating Simonson and Yoon's study for your own products and media options could lead to a dramatic difference in the way people feel about your brand.

With such diverse and intermingling influences shaping consumer behavior excluded from the market research process, it is perhaps unsurprising when its conclusions are wide of the mark. When McDonald's developed the Arch Deluxe burger in the mid-1990s, the company was confident that it had a winning product that would appeal to adult consumers. In the context of its market research the product performed very well, but in the context of a McDonald's restaurant, complete with "Happy Meals," Ronald McDonald, and other child-associated cues, the reaction was very different. Ironically, the advertising concept, which featured Ronald McDonald taking part in more grown-up activities, probably reinforced the contradictory associations customers were battling with.[14]

The corporate desire for control and standardization is understandable. It could be argued that it is essential to success for certain functions like accounting, procurement, and branding. However, as McDonald's discovered, centralized processes don't always offer the answer. When it comes to market research, the desire for a steer on development away from the complications of the retail environment are extremely risky. Devoid of the context in which it will eventually be sold, consumers can't respond authentically to a product. McDonald's developed its "Burger with the Grown-up Taste" from its Oak Brook headquarters in a direct move to appeal more to adults. Away from the plastic seating, bright primary colors, and menus of familiar, child-friendly alternatives, respondents rated the product highly for taste, freshness, and satisfaction. Despite more than $200 million of expenditure, at least $100 million of which was spent promoting this product that research had shown was so appealing, it failed and was withdrawn. According to one source, most of McDonald's successful product innovations, including the Big Mac, Fillet o' Fish and Hot Apple Pie, were invented in operators' kitchens, not remotely at head office. While these franchisees may not have had "robust" survey methods with which to research their inventions with customers, they could at least test their products in the environment in which they would be eventually be sold.[15]

All human behavior is heavily influenced by the environment. As Kevin Hogan, author of *The Science of Influence*, says:

> *Humans, like animals, interact with and respond to their environment far more than we are aware of at a conscious level. If you want to change your own or someone else's behavior,* the first thing you can do is change the environment. *Changing the environment is uniquely powerful in changing behavior. There is no greater single influence.*

Psychologist Stanley Milgram conducted a pioneering and now famous study on how context can change behavior, illustrating very powerfully that what people are prepared to do can change dramatically when the environment alters. The context can determine not just how the person behaves, but how differently they act from the way they might have expected to, and, in most cases, how they would like to tell themselves they would. In his experiment, 37 out of 40 participants administered potentially lethal 450-volt electric shocks to another participant in the test, simply because an apparently authoritative person in a well-regarded university's science lab asked them to do so.[16] (In fact, the person being shocked was in on the experiment and was only acting out the pain from the electricity the participants thought they were delivering.)

In the Stanford Prison Experiment, psychology professor Philip Zimbardo collected a group of students and assigned them at random to be either prison guards or prisoners in a mock jail that he'd created. Before the experiment was concluded (eight days early, after the intervention of the psychologist's girlfriend who had been brought in to conduct some interviews with participants and objected to the conditions that had developed in the mock prison), the guards had attacked prisoners with fire extinguishers, refused them access to a toilet, made them sleep on concrete floors, and subjected some to sexual humiliation. The experiment only lasted six days.[17] These dramatic examples are more extreme than anything market research is likely to encounter or create, but they illustrate the psychological principle involved.

When Mattel decided to introduce a new version of Barbie's companion Ken in 1993, it asked its target audience, 5-year-old girls, how they wanted Ken to look. The result was almost certainly a reflection of what girls of that age regarded as iconic of attractive masculinity at that time: boy bands. The groups often had gay impresarios or stylists and were happy to target the gay movement that was so vibrant as it worked actively to establish itself in mainstream life.[18] The resultant "earring" Ken doll wore a lavender mesh top with matching faux-leather sleeveless jacket, had two-tone frosted blond hair, and sported a small silver ring on a choker that was swiftly identified as a cock ring (a popular adornment of gay clubbers at the time).[19] This wasn't something most parents were happy to buy for their children; nor, once it had been pointed out, was it an image Mattel was happy to be associated with, and the doll was hastily withdrawn.

The artificial nature of the research environment can also be responsible for not flagging up something that, in the real purchase environment, is unconsciously reinforced and hugely significant in determining a product's fortunes. When Heinz developed All Natural Cleaning Vinegar it was a logical concept: the company already knew that people used their "eating" vinegar for cleaning and media interest in more natural cleaning products was high. Away from the context of the supermarket, a specific Heinz cleaning product seemed like a good idea. However, in the environment of a supermarket and, in particular, the context of the company's food products, it was hard for consumers to reconcile those unconscious culinary associations with those of cleaning products that they associated with dangerous chemicals and germs; the product failed and was withdrawn.

Often the influence of the environment on behavior is so subtle as to be imperceptible. Aron and Dutton set up an experiment involving two groups of male students.[20] Ostensibly the purpose of the research was to examine the impact of scenery on creativity; however, an attractive female interviewer was asking the questions and the two groups were in differing locations. The individual interviews for the first group took place on a wobbly bridge over a deep ravine; the second group were located on a bench on the other side of the bridge. The researchers were in fact interested to see how many of the participants asked the researcher out on a date. The difference was dramatic: 60% of those interviewed on the bridge telephoned the interviewer; just 30% of those on the bench did so. The researchers concluded that the people on the bridge misattributed their psychological arousal from the unstable bridge to the girl. Put another way, they knew they felt something, and their conscious mind wrongly diagnosed the sensation as a feeling of attraction to the researcher standing in front of them, rather than the fear of falling to their deaths from an unstable bridge.

Something similar was probably a significant factor in the failure of Peugeot's 1007 car.[21] When it was initially revealed as the "Sesame" concept car at the 2002 Paris Motor Show, the positive public reaction led the company to build and launch it; according to Peugeot's 2005 annual report, the "creative design delighted" executives. Whether the reaction was attributable to the novelty of the car's sliding doors, something Peugeot or another manufacturer was doing to generate excitement around its stand at the show, or the general buzz of the motor show is impossible to identify at this distance. However, the poor sales since the model was launched suggest that the positive reaction people thought was attributable to the new small car was misattributed excitement from something else going on at the time.

Creating the appropriate mood *around* a product – be it by staging an exciting event, wrapping a "hot" celebrity around it, giving it to people when they're having fun doing something else, or making them feel they've got a great bargain – can boost a brand's appeal precisely because of the phenomenon of unconscious misattribution. Experiencing a powerful feeling at the same time as experiencing the product can be sufficient to make the less rational part of our mind perceive something in a way that it otherwise wouldn't.

The virtual environment

Online retailers have the luxury of being able to conduct live trials that enable them randomly to assign customers to one of two or more alternative page layouts or even entirely different website designs. This gives them both a large degree of control over what a customer experiences and an opportunity to explore how subtle alterations to the environment change behavior.

The challenge with so much flexibility is to know what to test. It is apparent from studying what has been successful in such tests that, unsurprisingly, the same unconscious preoccupations shape how people respond online as they do elsewhere. There are still people who won't buy online because they feel it is too risky. However, most of us have evolved through a process of finding that an item we wanted was only available online or else was offered at such a discount there that we took the chance. The importance of feeling secure about buying online, particularly from a retailer that you haven't used before or that doesn't have a familiar high-street counterpart, has led to numerous protection schemes springing up. Their importance is evidenced by one website design test for luggagepoint.com, which that found sales increased by 5% and revenue per customer 11% when it moved the "Hacker Safe" crest a couple of inches to the right and removed a small banner next to it that promoted international shipping.[22] I can still remember the fear I felt buying a guitar from the United States on eBay in the days before PayPal protection existed. My anxiety was heightened by the fact that the seller insisted in typing his emails in capital letters. This relatively unusual ignorance of the Caps Lock key heightened my worry that he was a fraudster. Eventually, frequency renders such experiences mundane, at which point what matters is

that our expectancy of speed and simplicity is met. eBay tells me
that I've now bought 70 times – I had no idea.

A lack of ease, or fluency, can be a cause of lost sales. Where
customers can't find what they want easily, and even when the first
page of a site is slow to load, they will go elsewhere. One study
has suggested that, unless there is something on screen telling people that information is being loaded, two seconds is as long as people are willing to tolerate before they will move off.[23] Google found
that by making the Google Maps website faster (it reduced the size
of the page by around 25%) traffic increased by 10% in the first week
and by 25% just three weeks later.[24] I strongly suspect that the
specter of the unconscious mind's capacity to misattribute feelings
is at the heart of this phenomenon: mild frustration at waiting for
a page to appear can easily be felt as a dislike for what is on offer.

I now buy items online from my phone in the television ad
breaks without the slightest concern. What was once a source of
anxiety has been made fluent by Amazon's one-click order process.
I strongly suspect that many of the products I buy from the site
would be available more cheaply from its online competitors, but
it has made buying so easy I've never taken the time to check.
While a sufficiently discounted price is a reason to take a risk on
buying from somewhere new, it often doesn't determine subsequent behavior, when factors such as fluency (habit) and social
proof take over in importance. A 2001 study based on click-through
analysis of North American web users found that only 8% were
aggressive price hunters.[25]

Social proof, in the form of bestseller lists, testimonials, or
customer reviews, is also a hugely influential factor. Retail clients
tell me that those products that have the best reviews will sell best;
it's no surprise that, in the absence of seeing what other people are
buying, such information is important to online customers.

Conscious invention and selective recollection

Just as with Moll's plant wrapper (see Chapter 1), the fact that so
many studies show that people are unaware of how the environ-

ment and context affect their behavior and attitudes doesn't deter them from offering an apparently credible justification for what they do and why they do it. However honorable conscious intentions might be, consumers can't help but create and perpetuate myths about why they buy what they do when the researchers' questions are asked.

In a local department store I watched as a large number of passing customers stopped to look at a display for a new iPod speaker system. The display included the iPod and was pumping out music, making it hard to ignore. I approached several of the people to ask whether they had been considering buying this particular system prior to seeing it in the store; almost three quarters of them said they had. However, since I knew that the system was new and recognized the "foraging" consumption style in the store, I doubted that so many knew it existed. I changed the subject and talked about the product's features for a few minutes. When I asked these people later where they had first seen the speaker system, most of them said, as I suspected, that they had seen it in the store that day for the first time.

When I was researching the purchase of instant-win lottery scratchcards, respondents liked to believe that they bought them impulsively. However, I discovered a strange dimension to this impulse. When someone walked straight up to the newsagent's counter to buy something they would often not buy a scratchcard, but when they were required to stand in a queue they would. The unit that displayed the scratchcards was positioned in such a way that customers only saw the side when they were actually at the counter. The Perspex holder displayed the side of the cardboard reel of the scratchcards, not the eye-catching designs with the distinctive silver panels and references to the cash prizes. When there was no queue customers were less likely to be visually prompted by the card display and consequently less likely to buy one; queues created the visual opportunity to notice the scratchcard unconsciously, and the sight of it triggered associations in some people that they interpreted as a desire to purchase.

Combined with the inability to acknowledge accurately what aspects of our surroundings have influenced our behavior is our capacity to be selective witnesses. It's troubling to learn that a US study found that false eye-witness testimony contributed to three quarters of convictions that were overturned by DNA evidence.[26] Psychologists at Iowa University faked a crime in front of students and asked them to identify the perpetrator from five suspects, none of whom was the actual thief; 84% of students were willing to point the finger at one of the innocent suspects. This increased to 90% when they were told that one of the five had confessed to the crime and their claimed confidence in the identification increased from 6 to 8.5 out of 10.[27]

People are just as unreliable as witnesses of their own experiences. In 1991 James Randi, a challenger of the paranormal, conducted an experiment with the British medium Maureen Flynn. One of the tricks mediums use is to throw out huge numbers of names (or a few names with a large audience) to find a connection. Some time after the experience, he asked a client of Ms Flynn, who considered her reading to have been "very good," how many names she had mentioned during the 30 minutes the "reading" lasted. The client estimated that the medium had provided about six names. A transcript of a recording, however, revealed that she had mentioned 37 names, along with the initials N and L (which would provide a link to approximately 300 more).

The problems of context are further compounded by the time between the actual moment of interest to market research and when a question is asked about it. Wegner, Vallacher, and Kelly conducted an experiment to explore changes in how people define their actions over a period of time by interviewing people who were getting married. In advance of the occasion, they would often describe the event in romantic terms; closer to the occasion, they described it in terms of the details that were concerning them (such as getting flowers, wearing particular clothes, and so on); some time after the wedding, they tended to talk in terms of "getting in-laws" or "becoming a member of a family."[28]

As I said at the beginning of this book, humans have an extraordinary capacity for seeing things in a distorted way. We'll convince ourselves that a superstition or alternative therapy works, even though we've experienced numerous instances when it has failed to bring about the consequence we believed it had the power to influence. This trait, known as confirmation bias, also enables us to ignore our own apparently contradictory behavior. We can chastise a child for swearing and ignore the fact that, when we struck our thumb with a hammer earlier in the day, we used exactly the same language ourselves. Usually, no one is paying sufficient attention to point out our flagrant inconsistency, but once in a while an event occurs and it is exposed.

In 2007 an article in the *Daily Telegraph* magazine recounted the story of William Barrington-Coupe, who had passed off recordings of other classical musicians as those of his wife, Joyce Hatto – a pianist in her own right, but by that stage an infirm septuagenarian.[29] One twist in this tale involved the review that one of Hatto's "recordings" had received from the *Gramophone* critic Bryce Morrison in 2006. The article reports that he described her playing on a Rachmaninov Concerto as "stunning... truly great... among the finest on record... with a special sense of its Slavic melancholy." However, 15 years earlier the same critic had described the same performance (albeit performed under a different name) by saying that "(the performer) sounds oddly unmoved by Rachmaninov's intensely Slavonic idiom... devoid of glamour... lacks crispness and definition." There was no suggestion that the critic was doing anything untoward. A myriad of factors may have influenced his perception of the track on that day: the excitement surrounding this prolific new pianist, an earlier argument with a colleague, a change in his hearing, the impact of other music he had played beforehand, the music system he was playing the recording on, the temperature of the room, the packaging of the CD, the recommended retail price, even the smell of it. One thing is certain: his well-considered, well-intentioned, professional critique was markedly different, but the music was identical. It's tempting to suggest that his self-contradiction makes Morrison a bad critic, when in fact all we should really take from his unfortunate experience is that he is human and as susceptible as the rest of us to the subtle but significant influence of context.

Market research is gathered in whatever way seems most convenient; retailers don't want clipboard-laden interviewers harassing their customers. But what chance is there of getting reliable market research if the environment changes how people think, feel, and act? And, given what we know about our inability to access the workings of our own unconscious mind, respondents won't know they are being influenced and therefore can't possibly report them or attribute their behavior accurately to them in research. The locations used to label the noncontextual collection point of market research (online, in-street, and so on) should be seen as health warnings of the inherent unreliability of their findings.

The place to understand consumers is when they are in their natural habitat, wherever their unconscious mind is being exposed to everything that might shape how they feel. And the good news is that we can learn a lot from watching what consumers do.

4

WHAT CONSUMERS DO

Studying Behavior

Ask anyone why they have bought something and they will almost certainly give you a "good" reason for making the purchase. Take clothing, for example. Perhaps they bought a shirt because they liked it, they needed a new one, or they had a special occasion coming up and wanted to look their best. All of these seem fair enough, and certainly more reasonable than suggesting that they purchased the shirt because a salesperson said "Hello" or because the changing rooms in the shop were pleasant. However, by now perhaps you won't be surprised to hear that both of these have been shown significantly to increase the likelihood of someone purchasing a product. Paco Underhill, who has spent a lot of time observing shopping behavior in the US, suggests that the proportion of customers actually deciding to buy increases by half when there is staff-initiated contact with a shopper, and doubles when the shopper makes use of a store changing room.[1]

As I said in the previous chapter, the problem for organizations using market research is twofold. First, those research techniques that, by definition, take consumers out of context – the hall, street, home, viewing facility, or internet – are used for convenience and dismiss the crucial unconscious influence the environment has on what people think and do. Secondly, each presents a context of its own that will influence further the responses people provide. Those methodological labels for research should be seen as a health warning: *These results have been taken out of context.*

The potential importance of the environment is a powerful argument for conducting live trials (later I'll explain why, because of the issues questions raise, it isn't adequate simply to move existing research technique into the places we shop) and online split tests. However, they also provide a useful clue to how other useful consumer insights can be obtained. If people think, feel, and (most critically) behave differently in different environments, if they behave differently depending on who is present at the time, and if the unconscious mind screens the environment in such a way that people are unknowingly influenced by it, the place to understand them is in their natural habitat. Observing consumer behavior provides the opportunity to leave all these environmental variables in the mix in the quest to understand consumers better. Whether it is a desire to understand consumer thinking with the goal of developing better products or communication, or the need to get a better understanding of why a particular initiative is or isn't working, consumer behavior can be very revealing.

Reading the environment

According to researchers from Penn University, the human eye can transmit approximately 10 million pieces of information per second. Regardless of the mind-boggling quantities of data involved, anyone who has ever spent any amount of time looking for something, and then found it in one of the places they had already checked, will know that there is a big difference between what is there to be seen and what we actually notice. The highest estimates suggest that the most we're able to process is around 40 pieces of information per second (from all our senses, not just visually), so you can forgive yourself for not finding those keys first time around![2]

It's likely, if you pay close attention the next time it happens, that the first you're aware of seeing a fly buzzing around your face is as or just after you move your head or raise your hand in its direction; the unconscious scans and reacts, and consciousness follows. Just as the studies on magazine adverts and subliminal odors referenced previously show, this dual level of mental activity isn't always integrated accurately. The unconscious mind reacts to what is around and adapts behavior without necessarily revealing why. It shouldn't make any difference to a person's assessment of a set of cutlery that it is shown to them with a work of art alongside, but researchers discovered that people rated the cutlery as more luxurious when the artwork was there; the same happened with soap dispensers and bathroom fixtures.3 Of course, none of the people taking part believed that the apparently coincidental presence of a picture was affecting their judgment. They were unaware that their associations with art were activated and made them more likely to head down the neural paths for similar values when they considered the household items being shown to them.

So if you want to understand why consumers are acting in a particular way, it is important to be able to read the environment as a consumer's unconscious mind does. This involves observing what is there and accepting that, however peripheral it may be, it could be contributing to the way consumers behave. Light levels, ambient noise, odors, peripheral products, colors, music, interior design – whether they are artificially created or naturally present, all may influence how someone feels and what they choose to do.

Sometimes just an appreciation of these potential influences and comparing them is sufficient to provide powerful hypotheses about what is or isn't working. One client of mine asked me to investigate a competing retailer to help understand why consumers so often talked about them in such exalted terms. It was fairly easy to establish that the claimed excellence in customer service wasn't always borne out and that many people weren't even consciously aware of aspects of the competitor's offer (such as its price guarantee) that my client thought were important. However, the contrast in the store environments was enormous. One (my client's) bombarded customers with the level of white noise (generated by the air-conditioning system) that is normally reserved for inducing stress in physiological studies, and had fast-tempo, aggressive music playing; the other was an oasis of calm. One placed established brands to the fore with care and elegance; the other stuffed the aisles with unknown brands of budget lines in tatty boxes before the higher-quality products could be seen. Even if a customer were to buy the same product at a better price and receive more informed service from my client's store, it is likely that they wouldn't feel great about it because they couldn't feel great in that environment.

On other occasions it will be necessary to build on the understanding we now have of what environmental factors are known to influence customers and to compare the impact on sales and behavior when these elements are changed.

Consumer behavior: Nothing but the truth

At its most basic level, behavioral "data" is truth. It is what someone really does in a given situation. When the veneers of intent and self-justification are removed from the equation, what remains is what actually happens. With the single caveat that the subject doesn't know he or she is being observed – and so doesn't consciously or unconsciously modify his or her behavior – what occurs is the result of the conscious and unconscious processes at work in the individual's mind at the time. Whatever unconscious associations are being triggered by the environment, and whatever mood results from what each consumer has experienced and experiences in that context, are present to influence the behavior that takes place.

Of course, while accurate observation will tell you exactly *what* is occurring, *why* requires a degree of inference. That said, at least the focus of attention is entirely in the right area of consumer activity, and not reliant on someone's own assessments and postrationalizations of their experiences, as would usually be the case in market research. When the philosopher Bertrand Russell said "the discovery of our own motives can only be made by the same process by which we discover other people's, namely, the process of observing our actions and inferring the desire which could prompt them," he was commenting on personal introspection, but the implicit point about the benefits of observing others is worth noting: there is much to be learned from consumer behavior if you understand what it can reveal.

The benefits of observation over questioning (of both other people and oneself) have been illustrated by social psychologists. Self-perception theory goes so far as to suggest that we develop many of our attitudes and feelings as a consequence of observing our own behavior in different situations.[4] My son's dislike of dogs certainly isn't based on a conceptual dislike of hairy four-legged beasts, but a result of the fear he experienced being chased and knocked down by an overexuberant and badly trained bulldog at a neighbor's house when he was 2. Even at the age of 6 he still exhibits evident discomfort when he becomes aware of a dog and if you ask him, as I just have, he frowns and says: "I don't like them." However, in time, if we were to get a dog or if he spent a lot of time with a friend's, he could become far more comfortable around dogs. He would find himself reacting with fondness rather than aversion and at some point, if asked, might well say: "I don't mind dogs" or "I quite like dogs." I suspect that no amount of rationalizing about dogs is going to lessen his discomfort around them – and I have certainly tried to reassure him – but when he sees himself at ease his attitude will change.

In some ways, overweight people tell us all we need to know about the frailties of market research and the benefit of observing behavior. Many of them hold genuinely positive intentions about reducing the amount they eat at some point or another. Many believe quite strongly that they *will* lose weight by a given point in the future. Some will confidently state that they *don't* overeat or consume foods known to be highly calorific. Many start off on specific diet and exercise plans, often purchased at considerable expense, with a clear sense of purpose that they will change their ways. When the pounds aren't shed some will be incredulous, believing that they have followed a prescribed weight-loss plan and that, quite simply, "diets don't work" – to lose weight, their bodies need something beyond decreasing the ratio of calories consumed to calories expended. And yet, if your company's profits depended on it, would you rather rely on their claims, however rigorously interrogated, or the opportunity to observe how these people actually behave in relation to food? It's self-evident that we would learn everything we need to know from covertly observing the quantity, content, and frequency of their consumption.

As I will discuss in a moment, there are certain things to keep in mind when observing behavior in order that objectivity be retained. As you'll see, there are certainly ways of dramatically enhancing what can be gleaned from a behaviorally based approach to consumer understanding, but it is also the case that we're generally quite good at making accurate assessments of other people's behavior. Epley and Dunning conducted several studies exploring this. In one they asked students whether they would buy a flower for charity and whether they thought other people would; only around half of those who had said they would buy a daffodil did so, a proportion much closer to the average estimate of what they had said other people would do.[5]

It is well documented that people tend to have an overly positive view of themselves; although this is potentially of psychological benefit, it makes them unreliable reporters of their own actions. Generally, we like to see the best in what we've done, what we are doing, and what we believe we'll do in the future. It is also the case that other people are more likely to agree about what another person is like than they are to agree with that person's own assessment of themselves; the observations of others, even of our personality traits, aren't as subjective as we might like to believe they are (especially when we're being criticized).[6]

"Clean" observation

When it comes to studying consumer behavior there are two basic requirements if the research "process" isn't going to influence the outcome. The first, and easiest to achieve, is the need for observation to be covert: when people know they're being watched they become more self-aware, more self-conscious, and are likely to change what they do as a result (a point that I'll discuss in more detail when I consider the folly of the "viewing facility"). Suffice to say, the benefits of behavioral observation are significantly reduced if people are aware that their actions are being scrutinized or monitored.

Second, and a little more challenging, is the issue of observational objectivity. Undoubtedly the biggest risk with observation is confirmation bias, the tendency only to see or attribute relevance to the observations that fit with or confirm one's preconceptions.

One way to remove the potential for observer bias is to separate the observing and inferring aspects of the process. When observers are focused purely on recording what's happening, there is far less chance of them jumping to particular conclusions about what they see and then unconsciously filtering out subsequent evidence that conflicts with it. When it comes to observing behavior, while inference is of great importance, it should ideally follow a separate phase of observation.

So what should you look out for and what might it mean?

Physical behavior

Naturally, what people do is of primary interest. Not just what they end up buying, but where they walk, where they stop, what they touch along the way, and who they talk to. Collectively, these measures help to indicate the degree of engagement with any aspect at any point and the extent of interaction with it. Usually it is also relatively easy to identify how many alternatives form the consideration set from which the customer is choosing.

The most useful objective measurement is conversion: what proportion of the people who engage with something go on to purchase it? What proportion of the people who go into a store or a particular area within a store go on to make a purchase? How many people leave without buying anything?

An interesting indicator of consumer thought is time. Paco Underhill found that the amount of time someone spends shopping in a store (as opposed to waiting in a queue) is probably the most important factor in determining how much they will buy, and that the interception rate – the contact with staff from the store – is also crucial in determining the likelihood of a sale.[7] While neither of these statistics is particularly surprising, both are important behavioral measures; they are good examples of what can readily be observed, but they wouldn't be recognized or self-reported by a customer.

The amount of time people spend touching an object is also important and is a good indicator of their interest in it. In another of those studies that shows how the unconscious drives behavior, researchers found that when people held a product longer they were prepared to pay more for it. People were asked to bid on a coffee mug in an auction after inspecting it for either 10 or 30 seconds. On average, the people who had held it longer were prepared to pay 50% more for the mug.[8] So while holding a product may be the response to a desire on the part of the customer, or triggered by some aspect of the way in which the product is presented causing them to handle it, longer physical contact is a positive indicator of interest.

Walking pace can also be revealing. Comparing the walking pace of shoppers in different stores or different areas of the same store will provide a clear indication of how comfortable and relaxed they are. Are they moving slowly enough to be "open" to their surroundings, or are they marching through toward a particular target or to get away from somewhere uncomfortable?

Customers move at a very different speed if they are having a general browse and taking in the shopping experience as a whole. The faster they move, the more focused they are and the harder it is to get them to notice something other than what they've come to see. Recognizing where their pace changes can highlight the place in which to communicate the products or messages that you'd like your customers to notice.

If most customers move quickly from the entrance to a product or product category, that's indicative of the way in which they perceive the retailer or the product. Either the retailer is inherently not interesting to them (or worse, a necessary evil in the buying process) to the point that they'd rather not acknowledge where they are, or else the product is so essential that it is all they can think about; in most cases knowing the type of product concerned is sufficient to say which of the two applies.

Where customers reach for a product without significant conscious attention, for example they don't focus on the product as they select it, it is a strong indication that the purchase is familiar and straightforward; the unconscious is dealing with it at such a relaxed level that it will allow other sensory cues to be passed on. This is good news if it's your product they're selecting, but an indication of the massive challenge ahead if it's not and you're hoping to have them select your product in the future instead.

One retailer, keen to emphasize how competitive it was on price, put specially discounted products right by the entrance to its store, reasoning that customers would see them first and some would be encouraged to consider buying them irrespective of what they had come to the store for, so attractive was the level of discount. In practice, I could see that customers arrived at the store at a brisk pace, and that that pace didn't drop until they reached the category of products they had come to see. Even customers who had come to buy a product of a type that *was* being promoted near the entrance failed to notice it. Having reached the area inside the store that evidently contained the product type they had come to buy, it would have been quite strange behavior to start searching the store on the off-chance that one or two more might be located elsewhere; not surprisingly, none of them did so.

In the previous chapter I talked about mental fluency, the extent to which the unconscious mind likes to follow the path of familiarity. It is usually easy to gauge when the unconscious mind is running the show almost exclusively: a short amount of time spent watching customers will highlight the contrast between those who are running on an automatic pilot of sorts, and those who are engaged in more considered judgment. The amount of focused time given to one thing is an important gauge of the level at which mental processing is taking place. When actions happen quickly, it's indicative that the unconscious has learned how to take control of that process and regards it as risk free; the degree of consideration becomes indicative of how established the product or brand is in a person's mind.

When a customer takes your competitor's product without hesitating to consider alternatives, you learn a lot more about the strength of that individual's loyalty to the brand than you will get from attitudinal or preference ratings.

If someone tries to interact with a product, for example by pressing the buttons on a car in the showroom even though the keys aren't in the ignition, or pushes a finger inside a pack to touch a product, nothing could be expected to happen and nothing does. However, you will learn more about how product presentation and packaging can be improved than those people will necessarily be able to voice if you asked them. When I watched a customer pick up a large price ticket that was fixed into a plastic holder hanging from a shelf, I deduced that they were having difficulty reading the information and that either the simplicity of the list or the clarity of the writing wasn't as good as it could be. But when I asked the customer she had no recollection even of having touched the ticket, never mind of what her motivations might have been.

When US outdoor equipment retailer REI developed a new store, it spent a long time fine-tuning the design on a large scale in a warehouse, but it still knew that the only true test was to evaluate how customers responded in reality. It didn't just look at the sales figures, it spent time watching how customers behaved in the pilot store. One key aspect of the REI brand is that it works as a cooperative: customers become members and millions of dollars are donated to support conservation efforts that are intrinsically close to the hearts of the people who shop there. One way in which this cooperative spirit is embodied in the stores is through a community room. Rather than have this as a peripheral element of the building, the new design placed the room at the heart of the store – elevating it by a few feet to highlight the space. However, REI saw customers hesitating before going up the stairs, and realized that they were unsure if these led to a public area or not. In the next version the company repositioned the community area so that customers would pass through it naturally as they shopped.[9]

Making choices

Observation can also help identify the consideration set that people are using and, in the case of large-scale choices, whether they are managing to negotiate the different factors at all. In Chapter 1 I referenced the jam-tasting study that found that more people would buy from a smaller number of choices, just one of many that have shown how influential the number of options presented can be in determining the outcome of a person's experience when presented with a range of alternatives.

It's worth mentioning that choice isn't simply a matter of the number of options available. How readily they can be segmented, the number of data points for each option, and the density of the alternatives – how similar they are to one another – will also determine how easy or difficult it is to select from them. Buying a DVD from a supermarket is much easier than buying one from a specialist store because the range is much smaller. A manufacturer might have 50 different models when engine size and door configuration are taken into consideration, but if you know you want a mid-size family car from one manufacturer choosing is straightforward: one or two models with a few variants in each.

Generally speaking, we are more likely to buy when the range (or subset) is smaller, because one option is more distinctly identifiable as meeting our needs. Studies show that people feel more satisfied with a choice made from a smaller number of options; they have less anxiety that one of the other possibilities might have been a better alternative. It has also been demonstrated that people may perceive a range as bigger when it is smaller: there comes a point when the range is too extensive to perceive accurately and people underestimate the choices available. Since we tend to believe that more choice is a good thing, it's hard to acknowledge when we can't cope with it. In such cases we are more inclined to rationalize our feeling of difficulty in choosing by telling ourselves that what's on offer isn't very good than to acknowledge that we're not capable of making a decision.[10]

Observing which products people are choosing between can also reveal the consideration set they have found or else have created for themselves. Since, as I discussed previously, most judgments are relative, the way in which a purchase has been evaluated will be heavily influenced by the frame of reference within which someone considers it. There is good evidence that people tend to avoid risk by avoiding extremes. Of course, we all like to believe that we buy what we buy because we want to buy it, and that such a decision happens in the peaceful isolation of our own judgment; but thanks to the unconscious mind that isn't the case.

Again, it's the Nobel Prize winner Daniel Kahneman and his associate Amos Tversky (who demonstrated loss aversion) who we have to thank for identifying and confirming this phenomenon experimentally, and for creating the phrase "extremeness aversion."

They conducted a number of experiments in which they asked people to make a consumer choice and varied the number of alternatives on offer (as usual with such experiments, the people taking part had no idea what was being tested).[11] In one scenario they contrasted the proportion of people who chose to buy a $240 Minolta camera when it was offered with one (cheaper) alternative Minolta camera and when it was offered as the middle option of three; the proportion of people choosing the camera increased from 50% to 67%. In another experiment with Panasonic microwave ovens where a lesser brand was included as the base option, selection of the mid-priced product increased from 43% to 60% when a premium Panasonic microwave was included, and the brand's market share increased from 43% to 73%.[12]

In my own work I've found that not only is there a tendency for people to select a middle option of three or one of the middle two options of four choices, but also that they will make an effort to construct a situation where they give themselves a small number of alternatives from a much wider selection to make this possible. Observation helps show where and how consumers are doing this and provides an opportunity for companies to influence how they are referenced, through in-store positioning, packaging, and communication.

Making choices is a matter of finding the balance between the feeling of having a reasonable set of options to choose between and being able to manage the task. I've observed customers so overwhelmed by the degree of choice on offer that they didn't even try to look at it all before walking out of the store. Sometimes, the desire to put everything in front of the customer simply masks what's actually there. The same can occur with websites, which need to strike a balance between the number of products they can offer and the number they actually put in front of a customer at any one time. When faced with a large amount of information our reaction tends to be to scan reflexively, rather than to study everything more carefully. This was highlighted when the diet and exercise tracking website Daily Burn tested alternative designs for its homepage. Reducing the number of options that visitors could click on from 25 to 5 improved conversion by over 20%.[13]

Follow the eyes

It can be particularly important to know what people look at first when they are buying. In Chapter 2 I pointed out how susceptible we are to priming, attaching greater significance to what we see or hear first. Where customers glance first is of major importance because it can prime the way in which they perceive everything thereafter.

While knowing where people look provides no guarantee of knowing what they are mentally processing, it can be a useful reference point, especially when the amount of time is also considered. A fleeting glance is indicative of the unconscious mind reflexively scanning what it encounters; hypothesizing what associations it might have instantaneously connected to what it sees can be revealing. A longer look either means that more of the area has been reflexively scanned – an indication that they are searching for something that either is or feels familiar – or that one aspect (at least) of what they're studying is being referenced consciously in some way.

When a client was frustrated that people didn't seem to appreciate the freshly prepared food in his restaurant, I spent time watching where customers looked as they arrived. I realized that they saw the standardized décor, pre-printed menu, and familiar brand logo long before they encountered the handwritten "specials" board that listed the dishes created freshly that day. Customers were primed to think of the food offer as "standard" long before it reached their tables. It's important to appreciate that everything in the environment doesn't have the same impact, and that what comes first will have most significance in shaping what customers think about what they encounter later.

In another project, a retail client had invested in a new fixture for its store. The display was dramatically different from those around it and was placed centrally in the store, a few yards in front of the entrance. The aim was to increase sales of the products displayed on the new fixture (a category in which my client underperformed significantly), by making them an attractive focal point for people arriving at the shop, irrespective of what they had come to buy. Over time, it was hypothesized, customers' awareness of the shop as a supplier of these products would increase and that would drive up sales. Understandably, the retailer was keen to know what customers thought about the new fixture and installed one to test.

Ordinarily, the client's list of questions about the new investment would translate neatly into a set of questions that could be included in a qualitative discussion guide or quantitative questionnaire: Is the fixture attractive? Are the products well presented? Is it easy to handle the products? Is the information provided on the product tickets useful or sufficient? What would make the display better? All of the interested parties with the organization would want to know how their aspect of the fixture was working. However, there is a large degree of presupposition involved in all of these questions. Because the retailer has spent so long thinking about this display, because they believe it is so distinctive, and because it is so large and prominent in-store, it would be easy to presuppose the saliency and impact of the display to customers and, as you will now understand, the responses people might give about the display wouldn't necessarily reveal what they are really responding to and how. No customer is going to say: "Yes, the color used caused my unconscious mind to linger on the items therein triggering my conscious awareness; then the premium cues in the quality of the finish made me feel the items there were inherently high quality; I also saw other people stop and pick up items there and felt an instinctive urge to copy them." Nor were they going to say: "There's no point me telling you what I think about it, because I would never have noticed that large, distinctively colored, curved display the size of a badminton court that's right in front of the entrance."

By watching customers as they shopped in the store, and by not focusing solely on those who *did* interact with the fixture, a very interesting discovery was made: despite its apparent prominence most people didn't even notice the fixture – something supported by asking people if they knew whether the shop sold the products it displayed, where those were located, and even whether there was a curved, purple-colored display anywhere in the store they were walking out of. Tellingly, people had walked around the display without looking in its direction for long enough to have processed what they were seeing, and they didn't know that its products were available, where they were located, or even that the fixture itself existed.

When you are sufficiently familiar with behavior in a given context, you can infer a surprising amount from how long someone spends looking at something. Several years ago I was working in Turkey. My daily commute involved a 20-mile taxi journey from the Mövenpick hotel in Istanbul over the Bosphorus Bridge to a small industrial area called Tuzla. Unfortunately, the local taxi drivers seemed to regard me as an easy target for creative fares and routes to my destination; although I wasn't personally paying the bill, I took exception to being fleeced. Given that the only Turkish I'd managed to learn was "watch out!", "please," and "thank you," all for the benefit of the local taxi drivers, I wasn't well placed to argue my case. So I hit on the idea of asking the Turkish workers at the depot I was visiting each day to write a clear set of instructions for any taxi driver I should happen to get, including a line that specified how much I was prepared to pay for the journey. The first time I handed the sheet to a taxi driver I felt disproportionately pleased that I had regained control of the situation. But as we set off, I noticed that the driver was spending far too long looking at what was a very brief note and realized he was illiterate. Had it not been apparent to me immediately, it would have soon become so. I tend to think that the part of the journey where we were sailing the wrong way down the Bosphorus on a ferry would have given it away.

Back at that new retail fixture... I also saw that, on the rare occasions when people did stop to look at the products on display, they didn't stand there for very long. From my vantage point it soon became possible to hypothesize why: the display had an attractive convex shape that followed the line of the main walkway into the right-hand side of the store. The softer, carpeted flooring followed this curve, but only extended for a few inches beyond the display – not enough for anyone to stand on. As a result, people were effectively standing on the main "road" through the shop and, I surmised, felt unconsciously hurried by the pace of people passing them.

When it comes to evaluating promotional material or the effectiveness of packaging, testing the amount of visual attention an item receives can be useful in diagnosing the reason something hasn't generated the desired sales. If the item concerned isn't getting prolonged attention, the likelihood is that there is nothing about it the person associates with "interesting" or is sufficiently familiar with for it to be both recognizable and feel safe. It's worth being aware that visual communication has to attract the attention of the unconscious mind first, before there is the opportunity for someone consciously to appraise the message. It is the words, images, and colors that are of "importance" to the unconscious mind that will cause someone to take notice of something.

Recently I've been helping one client improve the impact of their in-store point of sale material – something I'd identified customers were frequently not engaging with. The new design they were trialing had two halves in different colors and it was apparent that people were only looking at one half of it. I suspect that their unconscious associations with colors and special offers were such that they would pay quite lengthy visual attention to one half, and even consciously engage with it, but disregard the other. In some cases one message was divided across the two colors; in these instances customers missed important information like the deadline for the deal or what product the discount related to. This inadvertent two-in-one trial enabled us to learn twice as much about what worked and what didn't.

Observing emotions

When it comes to understanding consumer behavior, the emotions displayed are particularly useful to observe. Of course, these emotions only exist in the "live" context of the experience that one is interested in understanding better.

It could be argued that emotions represent the best link between the unconscious and conscious minds. The fact that, as I have explained, it is not a particularly clear link within the brain and is frequently misinterpreted by the conscious mind doesn't prevent the emotion being expressed. It is interesting to note that, according to Joseph LeDoux, a professor at the Center for Neural

Science at New York University, the part of the brain that is primarily associated with emotions has a relatively meager connection with the part primarily associated with consciousness.[14] As Charles Darwin pointed out, while expressions can be sometimes be restrained by willpower, they are usually involuntary.[15] When they can be covertly observed from a dispassionate perspective, noticing what someone is doing, particularly when a shift in emotions occurs, can be very revealing.

Does the customer appear withdrawn, engaged, happy, anxious, or frustrated? Do the interactions with staff seem agreeable? When I watch a sales assistant greet a customer and the customer does not break stride and replies over his shoulder, it is apparent that the exchange has been initiated inappropriately or at an inappropriate time for that customer's comfort. When a customer shifts back away from a sales person's advance, only a basic ability to observe body language is required to note that she is not at ease.

It is possible to gain a good insight into the mindset of a customer (or anyone else for that matter) by closely observing their total package of "expressions." By paying attention to the words people choose to use, their tone of voice, the gestures, postures, and facial expressions, one can read with surprising accuracy the ego state (or frame of mind) they are occupying at any particular time.[16] The key is to observe the total package rather than erroneously attach significance to just one aspect and deduce, for example, that because someone has their arms folded they are feeling defensive (they may very well just be cold, feel more comfortable that way, or be unconsciously modeling someone else's behavior). Observing how someone's emotional state alters as they move through a retail experience, and identifying where a number of people respond similarly, is the key to identifying where an aspect of the retail experience is having an emotional impact.

The customer satisfaction survey is an excellent example of misguided thinking when it comes to market research. It presumes that a post-hoc, post-rationalized, conscious process can reliably gauge an experience that perhaps happened fleetingly, many days ago, and, most importantly, was primarily unconsciously filtered and processed. As the organization offering a service to customers, the business concerned has full access to the information it needs on how it's performing; that information is available every time someone interacts with the company. By carefully observing a sta-tistically appropriate random sample of service interactions, a robust perspective on how well the company is performing can be obtained and problem areas identified. I would argue that such an approach can provide much more accurate information about how customers feel than could ever reliably be established by asking them.

Given the problems of the fundamental misattribution error, whereby people mistakenly assign their feelings about one thing to another, detached observation can also make a judgment that a neg-ative customer reaction is disproportionate to the circumstance and potentially a reflection of aspects of that person's life that have nothing to do with the service being provided. As an extreme example, a hospital wouldn't be wise to remodel its Accident and Emergency service on the basis of the abusive drunks it has to deal with on Friday and Saturday nights.

Laughter itself is a very useful behavioral reference point. Most people can distinguish genuine laughter from artificially forced good humor if they put their mind to it. The former dean of Yale Medical School, Lewis Thomas, observed that moments of discovery were often accompanied by surprised laughter; when he heard laughter he would take it as a cue that there might be some-thing going on that was worth looking at.[17] If people are enjoying themselves it's generally a very good sign, scientifically and commercially.

As we get older we learn to be more sophisticated about what we see and how we see it. We are taught not to stare at other people. We project the values, prejudices, and insecurities we've acquired through the years onto what we see to reassure ourselves that we're right. The models that our unconscious mind has learned serve our basic needs, such as for parental approval (essen-tial to life when young) or personal empowerment. As a result, we lose the child's ability to see things as they really are; the social level of a situation conceals the real agenda of the person or people involved. When observing with the appropriate level of detach-

ment, it is possible to distinguish between the person who's genuinely happy and the person who is just saying they are as the
most socially acceptable way of ending the exchange.

Listening can also reveal a lot about how people are feeling.
Where there is the chance to hear what customers are saying to
each other or to staff, paying attention to their tone of voice and
choice of words can be very informative.

I was asked by a client to help them improve their telephone
call center customer service. As always when it's possible to do so,
I started by covertly monitoring the calls themselves (callers are
routinely told that calls may be monitored or recorded, so there
was no risk of the people I was listening to modifying their behavior because of my presence). In recent years it has become standard
practice to say to people calling customer service call centers: "Is
there anything else I can help you with?" Quite where this apparently reasonable question emanated from is unclear. It may well
have been voiced in consumer research as a means of suggesting a
great willingness to help, but a short time spent listening to the
response of one client's customers to it made clear to me that it
was not having the desired impact. The tone of voice of customers'
responses was frequently abrupt – an unhappy decline in the balance of the exchange suggesting that they were keen to get off the
phone (after what had often been an unwelcome call to have to
make in the first place). I also suspect that they were perfectly
capable of requesting further assistance if they needed it. The
nature of the exchange wasn't helped by the automated way in
which the offer was made; if you consider how wooden some
actors can make a line sound when they're saying it for only the
fourth or fifth time, it's perhaps not surprising that call center staff
who repeated it hundreds of times a week didn't imbue the words
with great passion or sincerity.

Watching how people follow the lead of others is also
instructive. In Chapter 2 I discussed the extent to which people can
be influenced by the reassurance of what they see people around
them doing. Watch a young couple walking down a street with
several restaurants looking for a setting for a romantic meal. They
will look at menus, but they will also look to see how full the

restaurant is; even if they're planning a quiet *tête-à-tête* they will usually avoid empty venues and choose one that is already being endorsed by other people.

Recently Professor Sam Shuster from Norfolk and Norwich University Hospital undertook a study that concluded that male jokes are a sophisticated form of aggression.[18] He discovered this when his unicycling through the streets of Newcastle upon Tyne invoked different responses from male and female onlookers. He started to record responses and found that they differed considerably according to age. Young boys and girls were both curious, but by the age of 11 boys became aggressive and tried to make him fall off his bike. In their teens, boys resorted more to disparaging jokes or mocking comments, and by late teens and early adulthood these became repetitive, funny putdowns concealing the aggression that younger males had expressed more openly. Older men were more amicable. By contrasting the responses by age and gender, Professor Shuster was able to hypothesize that the shifts in hormone levels through puberty might well account for the difference in response and even, ultimately, for why there are far more male comedians than female. Aside from being fascinating in its own right, the study reveals how useful behavioral observation can be; certainly there is no way I can think of that such an understanding could have been garnered by asking people how and why they used humor, or indeed how they would respond to the sight of someone on a unicycle!

When observing people's interactions with a customer service desk of a national retailer, it was apparent that the experience was horrendous for most of the people concerned. The staff ignored customers until the latter initiated contact and during the subsequent exchange the customer service representative spent most of her time looking at her computer screen, rather than giving the customer the level of eye contact one would normally see in human interaction. Some of the customers were evidently angry from the outset, no doubt irritated that a product was faulty and they had had to make a trip to the store to resolve it. However, others reacted to the curt and disengaged attitude of the staff by shifting from an emotionally neutral disposition to one of anxious defensiveness or anger. When another member of staff was required, the person behind the counter would shout across the customer toward the tills, and often the customer would physically recoil at the abrupt change of volume.

However, when I asked customers about the experience they had just had, most reported that they were satisfied with the encounter; a reaction that appeared to be entirely dependent on the fact that they had managed to get their issue resolved. When I asked them about their perceptions of the retailer in general, they were very negative about the company, how little it seemed to care about them as customers, and how poor its product knowledge was; these comments were totally in keeping with the uncomfortable exchanges I had just witnessed. While an exit poll would have reported high levels of satisfaction, the real issue was that the poor interpersonal experience was seen by customers as symptomatic of the brand as a whole: their expectations were so low that all that mattered was getting a satisfactory outcome. The customer service process simply reinforced shoppers' negative perceptions of the store (perceptions that the retailer was working hard to change elsewhere in its service). For a company struggling to improve the perception of its brand, it was far more informative to understand the customer service experience as a whole than people's self-reported assessment of it. In this case, the halo effect of one positive moment is perfectly capable of masking an experience that has reinforced existing unconscious associations.

Virtual observation

Short of surveillance techniques best left to government agencies, observing online customer behavior is not an option. However, there is a wealth of behavioral data readily accessible to internet retailers beyond the analysis of conversion data and sales. Identifying how long visitors to a site spend on each page, when considered in the context of the role that page is designed to fulfill, can reveal how well it is serving its function of helping them find their ultimate destination on the site and how engaging they find it when they get there.

Technology is providing new insights into what web users are doing, for example tracking the places visitors move their mouse and where they click, and summarizing it in the form of "heatmaps." Other software can record users' visits to a site and replay an entire customer journey in real time, and also bring such data together in aggregated reports. Such tracking happens covertly, ensuring that the information gathered is a genuine insight into behavior, rather than one influenced by conscious awareness of the research process or instigated in response to a request to look at the site and comment on it. Learning where online customers skip through content or that they fail to reach potentially important information at the bottom of a page can enable specific weaknesses to be identified.[19]

Believing what you see

Edgar Allen Poe is reputed to have said:

> You are young yet but the time will arrive when you will learn to judge for yourself. Believe nothing you hear, and only one half that you see.

When it comes to understanding consumers, I would suggest that's a reasonable rule of thumb. To paraphrase Poe, I'd suggest that we should believe nothing we hear from consumers, half of what we see them do, and almost everything that the sales data says they've done. So what evidence is there that asking people what they think is such a bad idea?

5

THE IRRELEVANT CONSUMER

Questioning questions

With the year 2000 approaching, countries around the world began considering how they might celebrate and commemorate this essentially arbitrary numerical event. In the UK an initial concept for a "World's Fair" showcase event was developed by Tony Blair's government into something much grander: someone hit on the idea of building the largest single-roofed structure in the world and putting some stuff in it that signified *Who We Are*, *What We Do*, and *Where We Live*. But at the end of its year-long life the Millennium Dome was widely regarded as a flop.

In 12 months, 6.5 million people visited an attraction that had cost the country more than £600 million.[1] This was 5.5 million people fewer than the original estimate and almost 20% below the "worst-case" scenario estimate provided by consultants Deloitte & Touche, who factored in "risk factors" like the possibility of the content being insufficiently attractive and marketing failing to pull in the forecast mix of visitors.[2] A subsequent review by the advertising agency M&C Saatchi entitled "Will 12 Million Visit the Dome?", based on NOP tracking research, concluded that the figure of 12 million was "conservative," given a pool of between 16 and 18 million people who had made statements that caused the research company to classify them as "likely" or "persuadable" visitors.[3]

To confuse matters somewhat, research conducted during the year the Dome was open found that 87% of visitors were "satisfied" with their visit, and 86% were "satisfied" with the services provided by the Dome's hosts; another survey found that "nearly all respondents were aware of the Dome."[4]

So where had it all gone wrong? The moment the organizers asked people about the Dome, they were on a slippery slope toward a 6 million person fall – because they were asking the wrong people.

I'm not suggesting that the research sampling was awry, rather that the people questioned by the research process had little or no connection with the ones who would ultimately make the purchase decision. To some extent this is a by-product of the issues raised in the previous chapters: someone's decision to visit the Dome is a balance of unconscious influence and the context at the time the decision is made. For example, when the idea was raised in research several years before it was due to take place, there was growing excitement about so many digits on the calendar changing simultaneously. But once January 1st had passed, the Y2K computer problem hadn't spawned Armageddon, and everyone had adjusted to a 1 and three 9s turning into a 2 and three 0s, life settled back into its familiar patterns. Making a trip down to a relatively inaccessible borough of a busy capital city with a poor transport infrastructure, to an "event" that was being regularly criticized (and no one was claiming *really* contained the "greatest show on earth" as the government had promised),[5] didn't seem like quite such an attractive proposition.

However, this wasn't solely a matter of not appreciating the Dome in its actual context. Additional surveys conducted by NOP in April and August 2000 suggested that 15 million and 12.4 million people "had already visited, are likely to visit or could be persuaded to visit."[6] With the folly of the Dome publically exposed, why were people still saying they would go when, as the year-end figures proved, they weren't going to? The answer is that the research interview process does more than merely ignore critical components of why people behave as they do, it changes how and what they think.

In a world where so much time and money is spent on market research in one form or another, there is every chance that, at some stage, a statistic or report will be pushed in front of you as justification for a decision. Concern about the quality of research tends to be focused on the validity of the sample and the statistical significance of any differences in the data, but as the Dome's experience illustrates, the statistical methodology can be pure and the results still grossly misleading. There are 13 reasons most questions should be avoided, which will be explored in this chapter.

1 Questions inadvertently tell people what to think about

Raising something as a question pushes it into the conscious mind for a conscious response. It frequently also makes a presumption about how relevant or interesting that issue is to the person concerned. In an understandable attempt to explore what someone thinks about something, the very fact that you ask them about that thing is a potential distortion of reality. For example, in asking how trustworthy I consider a brand (or yourself) to be, you presuppose that, at the moment of decision making, trustworthiness is an influential variable in the decision.

This point was illustrated by one of my clients when they asked me to help them understand whether their investment in a new store design was worthwhile. When they had tested a new store previously, they had used "accompanied shops"[7] to get customer feedback. The research had told them that the new store was a significant improvement and was very much liked by customers. However, when more stores were refitted and could be assessed in terms of their sales performance against the rest of the estate, the client could see no evidence of a financial return to justify the additional investment.

Unfortunately, the researchers' questioning during the accompanied shops had prompted customers to consider various aspects of the store, not least those in which the company had invested and on which they were keen for the research company to report back. These questions presupposed the importance and, indeed, existence of the new elements in the customers' experiences; as soon as the researcher asked about an element of the store, it was reasonable for the respondent to examine it, consciously appraise it, and reply.

I discovered that many of the new elements contained in the store went unnoticed by customers, and that key elements of the store that were unconsciously referenced during the retail experience had not been changed. In particular, customers scanned the perimeter of the store to navigate it, enabling them to retain one focal length as they scanned the environment, and ignored relatively large features that had been created in the middle of the store, but that were not relevant to their visit and didn't require referencing for navigation.

While this phenomenon can be hard for people to accept when they not only know what is there, but have taken the decision to invest a considerable amount of money to have it put there, it is well documented in psychology. Studies such as those by Simons and Chabris have proved that people often ignore apparently significant visual events if their attention is focused elsewhere (even a gorilla walking into a group of basketball players and beating his chest can be overlooked through so-called inattentional blindness).[8]

When you become conscious of other people's extraordinary capacity to fail to notice things, you become more aware of when you do the same yourself; though on the basis of my own experience, no better at combating it. Shortly after writing this passage I was searching eBay for a particular brand of golf club that I'm interested in buying. A seller had listed exactly the clubs I was interested in and I clicked on the listing to read more. There was relatively little information provided, just one picture and only four lines of text, amounting to thirteen words in a font much larger than the one that you're reading now. In addition the seller, who also operated an eBay shop selling unrelated products, had added a disclaimer that the golf clubs were a personal sale and, reassuringly, not a martial arts weapon.

After reviewing the information, I sent a short email to the seller to ask what condition the clubs were in; the picture resolution was too low to tell and I was a little concerned that this most basic information wasn't included. After sending the email I returned to the listing and, for some reason, looked at the information again (it is shown below exactly as it appeared in the advert):

Tour Edge Bazooka Iron-Wood
Reactive Flex Regular
5-9 PW SW
In excellent condition

I emailed the seller and apologized for my inattentional blindness!

It doesn't help the accuracy of research that, once they've agreed to take part, people are almost always helpful enough to answer the questions they're asked. However, all the responses provided are not the result of equal thought or awareness of the issue concerned. When people were asked if they thought the US government should spend money on an antimissile shield, the results appeared fairly conclusive: 64% thought the country should and only 6% were unsure. But when the pollsters simply added the ambivalent option in the question "...or are you unsure?" the level of uncertainty leaped from 6% to 33%! When they drilled down marginally below the surface and asked whether respondents would be upset if the government took the opposite course of action from their preferred route, 59% of people either didn't have an opinion or didn't mind if the government did something different; a far less compelling endorsement for spending all that money.[9]

The fact is that asking about something overrides the natural state that thing occupies in someone's experience. It's very hard to preempt what people will find interesting or attention worthy – which makes it very risky to presume by asking them a question about it. When research has put a focus on the issue it's investigating that causes people to consider it a way they otherwise wouldn't, it has manufactured the response it gets.

The way in which questions change mental processing doesn't only undermine the process of asking other people questions. Similar problems can arise when asking yourself a question about consumer experience that can lead you to arrive at erroneous conclusions, something that was demonstrated recently when I was observing customers to evaluate the impact of a new store design.

Over the course of a couple of days at the store (and from previous work for the client) I had had the opportunity to observe a large number of customers shopping there. While there were some important but subtle differences in response to the environment, for the most part people behaved in a very similar way. From my observation and subsequent interviews with a sample of them, I knew that people were usually in a very unreceptive mindset when they arrived, screening out large areas of the store and focusing (at least initially) on the specific product they had come to view. The store was located on a retail park and there was very little "passing trade" or browsing, since shoppers had to put a reasonably large degree of planned, conscious thought into the decision to travel there. Where the store design was successful, it did draw people into other product areas and entice them to look at and interact with other items, and I knew which these points were and how the location and design of the fixture and nature of the products had influenced this customer behavior.

On the second morning, two men walked into the store and behaved very differently. They started an unplanned but nevertheless systematic sweep of the whole store. They looked at everything: the signs, the lighting, and the carpets. It was easy to conclude that these people were not there to look *in* the store, they were there to look *at* it. Knowing of the intense rivalry that existed between my client and its main competitor, and on the basis of their appearance, I guessed that the men were senior managers from the competing retailer. I decided to try to "interview" them at the end of their visit.

When I asked if they would take part in some research, there was a momentary pause during which I suspect that the more senior of the two was weighing the chance of him learning things from me about his competitor against his irritation of taking part in the research. His professional curiosity won through and he agreed to answer some questions. His responses confirmed what I had already observed: he had appraised the store in a totally different way from a genuine consumer. He used commercial category terms and made comparative references to other stores around the country. He talked about lighting levels, signage, and the flow of the store, and he aesthetically appraised the new fixtures. Real consumers don't talk about any of these things and don't make any conscious evaluation of them during their purchase experience. Indeed, they are oblivious to most of them at a conscious level.

Unsurprisingly (at least to someone versed in the principles of transactional analysis), the conclusions the men came to based on their conscious, balanced (adult) assessment of the store's design had nothing in common with the reaction of real consumers. In many ways, as soon as they asked themselves the perfectly reasonable question "I wonder what that new store is like?" and decided to go and look in order to answer it, they were destined to misinterpret what they saw, at least in terms of how a consumer might have directly or indirectly appraised it. Consumers had a very different perspective, being preoccupied with conscious matters ("Have they got what I want?" and "Where is the thing I'm considering buying?") and unconscious matters ("Do I feel happy and safe here?" and "Do I feel in control?"). The two men had not seen the store as consumers saw it, to the extent that they may just as well have gone and looked at a different store!

2 Questions changing what people think

There is also evidence that simply asking people questions about something will change the answers they provide. Wilson and Schooler designed an experiment in which people were given a number of jams to taste that ranged in quality (on the basis of an expert taste panel) and asked to rate them. Some participants were asked for their reasons for liking or disliking each jam before rating it; others were given an irrelevant questionnaire first. It transpired that the people who consciously deconstructed their jam preferences devised criteria that were unlike those used by the experts, based their ratings on these reasons, and came to a different conclusion about which was best. In contrast, the group who weren't encouraged to think about the taste of the jam in this abstract and artificial way had preferences that corresponded very closely with the expert panel.[10]

We like the notion that our judgment is self-contained; it is after all our own judgment and it will be what it will be. However, research shows that our judgment is far more malleable than we might like to believe. Tormala, Petty, and Clarkson asked participants about their perceptions of a fictitious store that had been described to them in terms of three of its departments.[11] The store description was always the same, but the information participants were exposed to immediately prior to seeing it varied. What emerged was that, whether the information was about a competing store, a car, or a hypothetical person, the nature of that information affected the responses to the description of the department store. When the first message was sketchier and less informative, the department store was perceived more positively.

It is very easy to demonstrate just how influenced people can be by contextual information. If you ask someone to think of a number they will quite often say 7, and very often say a number between 1 and 10 (because that's a common mental association with the suggestion). However, if you ask someone to think of a number and first tell them that you yourself are thinking of the number 876, it's likely that they will come up with a three- or four-digit number of their own. You can demonstrate how apparently irrelevant information primes people in a similar fashion. Contrive a reason for someone to think of a larger number, for example by talking about how wide the Atlantic is, and then ask them to think of any number. For a linguistic example, you've probably heard the brain teaser that primes someone with a detailed story about a fatal plane crash involving people of two different nationalities that comes down on a border and asks in which country the survivors would be buried. Everyone knows you don't bury survivors. However, when the answer isn't obvious the unconscious is just as ready to latch on to any peripheral information available at the time and link a response to it, irrespective of its relevance.

Salespeople know that they can prime reactions to the price of their product by using larger numbers before they get to their "bargain" price. Similarly, consumers will flock to a discounted product, even without any absolute knowledge of the usual undiscounted price of the item.[12] When people have been thinking in terms of numbers at one numerical level, they use that as a base point from which to define another number.

It's also possible to be primed by the most trivial suggestion. While taking part in a charity rally with a friend of mine, I was bemoaning the fact that I had forgotten to buy new toothpaste and would have to eke out the remnants of a tube I had considered long since dead until we passed a supermarket or pharmacy. My friend echoed my concern, commenting that he only had a tiny tube supplied in a wash kit from an airline to last him the five days of our journey from the UK to Portugal; he had hoped the razor and toothpaste he'd picked up would last the trip, but now he wasn't sure. The following day it transpired that he hadn't got any toothpaste at all. Primed by a notion of what other airlines included in the travel kit and, presumably, the nature of the tube, he had brushed his teeth as planned. He thought it wasn't particularly minty or tasty toothpaste, but put that down to the airline's poor choice of supplier. In the morning, his mouth soured by a particularly unpleasant taste, he checked the tube again, only to discover that it contained shaving cream.

It seems that it is impossible to prevent this priming effect. When Kahneman and Tversky did their ground-breaking work on behavioral decision theory, they put numbers around numerical answers, for example from a wheel numbered from 1 to 100 that appeared to spin at random (in fact they were controlling the outcome), and observed that people's subsequent responses to questions with a numerical answer were influenced by the number to which the wheel had spun.[13] When Timothy Wilson asked people to guess the number of physicians in a phonebook, he offered a substantial prize, warned one subset of the participants that people could be influenced by numbers they'd seen in earlier questions when making estimates, and urged them to be as accurate as possible. Even under such conditions, when people might be expected to draw on all their rational resources, the estimates provided were influenced by irrelevant numbers placed in the preceding questions.[14]

How big a difference can priming make in surveys? David W. Moore, author of *The Opinion Makers* and a former senior editor at the Gallup polling organization, compared two polls looking at US citizens' support for oil drilling in Alaska's wildlife refuge. One found that the public was opposed to drilling there by a margin of 17 percentage points. The other, conducted within a month of the first, found people in favor of drilling there by exactly the same margin. (Both polls corresponded with the interests of the groups that had commissioned them.) The poll that found more people in favor of drilling preceded that question with 13 others about the cost of oil and the country's dependence on foreign suppliers. The poll that found more people against asked only the question on drilling in that region of Alaska.[15]

Psychologists have also found that the way in which people make evaluations about one set of products changes how they evaluate subsequent products. When a process has encouraged people to think about similarities or differences between brands, as is the case in a "market mapping"[16] exercise, it can fundamentally change how they think about another, unrelated product.[17] The way in which people think about the second product is, at least in part, defined by the previous exercise.

Similarly, several studies have found that the unconscious impact of one product, or series of products, influences the response to a subsequent product from an entirely different category. The same is true in response to advertising: where people looked at a basic product after seeing a premium one, they found it more appealing than when it was viewed in isolation.[18]

Recently researchers experimented by manipulating the difficulty of an article on movie reviews from a film festival that people were asked to read before looking at an advert for a watch. They discovered that if the article was difficult to read (something they manipulated by the type and size of font selected rather than the slightly more subjective adjustment of the content itself), people responded more favorably to a subsequent advert that was easy to process. It seems that, in the context of the difficult article, the positive relief of being able to understand the ad easily was inadvertently projected onto the advert. The research also discovered that when the advert had a connection to the content of the article, people liked the ad less even if it was easier to read. It seems that the unconscious associations between the company and the difficult article caused the reader to like the advertised product less too.[19]

It is eminently reasonable that research should want to make comparisons, be it of competing brands, different product formulations, or packaging options between which a company is choosing, or to get a relative position against its competition. After all, knowing that your company is "trusted" (whatever that might mean) by 65% of its target consumers is not as interesting as know-ing that your main competitor is trusted by only 41% of people. To achieve this, research has to present respondents with a number of different alternatives and ask whatever questions it considers inter-esting. Unfortunately, by imposing a number of options for the benefit of the research design, such research is creating an artificial dimension that can affect the responses it receives.

It would be good to think that whether we like something is a discrete and independent matter related only to our tastes; after all, in a sense we define ourselves by our choices and we may believe that we alone are in control of these. However, psycholo-gists have found that the range and nature of choice affect what people choose and how they feel about it. People given a wider selection of chocolates to choose between found the ones they ended up selecting less tasty, enjoyable, and satisfying than those given a more limited choice.[20]

The same issue arises in the question of what someone will choose from a number of options. When researchers asked people to choose between two cameras, a Minolta X-370 priced at $169.99 and a Minolta Maxxum 3000i at $239.99, 50% chose the X-370. However, when all they did was add in a third option, the higher-priced 7000i at $469.99, the proportion choosing the X-370 more than halved to 21%.[21] In another study, the addition of a second choice of CD player over a stand-alone product resulted in the proportion of people deciding to purchase a product dropping from 66% to 54%.[22]

In another study, three quarters of doctors presented with a new drug for osteoarthritis would prescribe it rather than refer patients to a specialist. When a second drug was presented as an alternative option, the proportion deciding to refer patients to the specialist increased significantly. The choice we make doesn't exist as an absolute, it's dependent on the number of alternatives available.

3 Inadvertently leading the witness

People are inherently open to suggestion. I'm not talking about the "hold up a security van at gunpoint," Derren Brown-style suggestion (although a small proportion of the population is that suggestible), I'm referring to the way in which we all unconsciously filter what's going on around us and feel a particular way as a result. For example, if someone asks you how your life will be different in five years' time, you could think about any aspect of your day-to-day existence and speculate on how it might change. However, if someone asks you how your life will be different but includes a prompt or two, perhaps by asking whether you will you be living in the same house and doing the same job, the probability that you will talk about accommodation and work is extremely high.[23] While it's unlikely (although not impossible) that such a question would be used by a good market researcher, this example illustrates an issue that can manifest itself far more subtly.

The unconscious mind, preoccupied as it is with rapidly processing and filtering lots of pieces of information, references countless aspects of our environment, including what it hears, and conditions us according to what it finds. A particular word or phrase triggers a set of associations: we get the unconscious reaction first and then consciously make sense of it (this is one of the reasons we're able to communicate so rapidly, and without knowing what we're going to say in advance). The consequence is that our decisions and responses become a by-product of what's been said and are not fixed personal values at all. Psychologists refer to this issue as framing and it doesn't just influence what we think in abstract terms, it influences what we do.

In one experiment, doctors, patients, and students were asked to choose between two forms of treatment therapy for lung cancer. They were given survival data on the efficacy of surgery and radiation; one group was given information on the probability of living, and one on the probability of dying. When the information was framed to tell them that people opting for surgery had a 68% probability of surviving beyond one year, surgery was chosen 75% of the time. However, when the question framed the data on the basis of mortality (i.e., 32% will be dead within one year) only 58% chose the surgical option.[24] Another study, which asked people to decide who got custody of a child in a divorce based on short descriptions of each parent, showed that the answer shifted significantly depending on whether the question asked who they would "award custody to" or who they would "deny custody to"; the simple change in wording swung the majority from one parent to the other.[25] Opinion polls have been found to be extremely sensitive to the choice of language used. For example, a poll is more likely to show public support for something when it frames the question as the government "not allowing" it rather than "forbidding" it.[26]

Unfortunately, problems are caused by *not* framing a question too. When research is asked in an abstract way it will lead to a different result from when more information is provided; it's easy to be in favor of something when you haven't considered the true cost and when the question doesn't prime you to consider it. Four polls asking about renewing and expanding the US State Children's Health Insurance Program (SCHIP) found support ranging from just 40% (52% were against) to 81%; the differences appeared to stem from different levels of explanation about the program, whether it was made apparent that there was a political divide in support for the bill, and whether the cost was mentioned.[27]

It's worth noting that the price of tickets to visit the Dome weren't announced until March 1999, two years *after* the research used to estimate visitor numbers.[28] However, even when allowances are made for people not having known the price of entry, the nature and quality of the attractions, and the critical reaction of the media, research conducted in August 2000 (by which point the Dome had been open for seven months) still put 12.4 million people in the classification "already visited, are likely to visit or could be persuaded to visit."[29]

4 The accidental sell

As much as researchers might like to believe that they are being dispassionate (and as I mentioned previously, it's questionable whether many actually achieve a genuinely noninfluencing questioning style), there is a very fine line between showing or describing to someone something that you want them to talk to you about and promoting it in their mind.

There is strong evidence to show that people are significantly influenced by how vividly information is presented. For example, when researchers presented a Save the Children appeal for African famine victims referring to the scale of the problem in statistical terms of the millions of people affected, only half as much money was donated as when the problem was depicted in terms of its effect on just one little girl.[30]

In a research setting, the focus on the subject matter created by being asked to stand and think about a particular issue, or by being presented with a description of a brand or product to appraise, is inherently artificial. However, it may also present the information in a way that shapes how people respond to it. The more detail you give respondents to consider, the more they will say. But in providing a vivid depiction of the brand, product, or service (or conceivably even when asking respondents questions that require them to construct such a depiction in their mind), another source of inadvertent influence has been introduced and the consumer responding is another step away from the one who will be making purchase decisions in the real world. It's easy to conceive of the way in which respondents created a vivid mental image of the Dome's "greatest show on earth" and convinced themselves that they would simply *have* to go and see it when it opened. Nevertheless, despite spending £40 million, the agencies tasked with attracting visitors were unable to recreate the same level of desire through their marketing efforts.[31]

Where the research has deconstructed or packaged the subject matter in an artificial way, it is impossible for it to be an accurate reflection of what people really think or do.

5 Inadvertently persuading people to like something

It's very common for qualitative research to ask what people like about a particular product. Any research appraisal of a product being developed is likely to ask a consumer, or group of consumers, their opinion of the product. Either overtly or because it is an automatic basis for *conscious* evaluation of something new, people talk about what they like and dislike in what they are being shown. While this may seem inherently balanced, since both the positive and negative are being sought, there is a risk that in searching for the positive and postulating it, respondents unconsciously alter their position favorably.

You might think that beliefs are inherently stable. People will go a long way for what they believe in; some people will even wrap themselves in explosives and die for their beliefs. Certainly, market research has been interested in beliefs for years and considers them the foundation that underpins attitudes. Questionnaires frequently include attitude statements with which respondents can agree or disagree; this provides a way of getting responses that go beyond the monosyllabic limitations of quantitative surveys, without incurring the cost of using open-ended questions that will later require categorizing into meaningful groups and proportions. Such questions are "wonderful" for researchers, because the necessarily loaded nature of the attitude statements ensures data on something respondents would probably not express in a structured survey.

However, social psychologists have shown that asking someone to talk about something can change their opinion about the subject matter. Janis and King found that rather than their being fixed, beliefs can be *created* through behavior. Participants who made a speech playing the role of someone who believed in a particular issue were found to have become believers in the issue itself afterwards.[32] In other words, the act of making the speech formed the "belief," rather than a prior belief being constant throughout the forced experience.

So when researchers ask "What do you think the company is saying about its product in this ad?", they don't realize that the process of respondents conceptualizing the message of the communication may predispose them to accept it.

More recent research by Shen and Wyer found that simply asking people to choose whether they would buy or reject each of a number of products encouraged respondents to search for favorable attributes before unfavorable ones, and resulted in them regarding the next product they saw more favorably than they otherwise would have done; the question itself primed people to think more positively.[33] Ultimately, the process of asking someone to evaluate something can change how they actually feel about it, or how they feel about another thing that you talk to them about subsequently.

6 Artificially deconstructing the consumer experience

Blind testing is a good example of a research technique that is commonly deployed to provide an "unbiased" understanding of how well a product performs in the mind of the people who might buy it while simultaneously failing to appreciate how those minds really work. The notion that a product tested without branding is somehow being more objectively appraised is entirely misguided (as Coca Cola discovered to its cost with New Coke). In the real world, we no more appraise things with our eyes closed and holding our nose than we do by ignoring the brand that is stamped on the product we purchase, the look and feel of the box it comes in, or the price being asked.

Our reliance on brands isn't an indication of some form of shallowness or lack of intelligence; it's a pragmatic system of packaging up product associations into an unconsciously identifiable device that removes the need to make complex and long-winded conscious evaluations of alternatives every time we purchase something. The fact that the system isn't perfect, and that we may end up buying a product that we had associated with one set of attributes that it turns out not to have, doesn't invalidate the approach most of the time, nor provide any practical alternative. A customer faced with hundreds of choices needs a way to filter what's available; the unconscious mental power we (usually) no longer need to guard against life-threatening animal attacks can be deployed to helps us get a decent tin of beans quickly.

Many of us would like to think that we aren't so shallow as to be unduly influenced by what's written on something, but recent research suggests that we're far more influenced than we might think. Researchers from Duke University found that even when brand logos were shown subliminally (flashed at speeds beneath conscious awareness), participants' subsequent behavior was changed in a way that reflected the established values of those brands. Comparing responses to creativity tasks after subliminally exposing people to either an Apple or an IBM logo revealed that people who had seen the former brand, associated with nonconformity, innovation, and creativity, devised more unusual and creative uses for an everyday object (in this case a brick). They conducted another test using the Disney Channel logo and the one for the E! channel[34] and found that people primed by exposure to Disney behaved much more honestly in subsequent tests.[35] Since none of these people knew they'd seen the logos involved, they couldn't have been consciously influenced by them and couldn't have explained their subsequent behavior in the tasks; as far as they were concerned, they were simply being themselves and behaving as they believe they typically would.

In functional magnetic resonance imaging (fMRI) research, German radiologists have found that brands can change the way people think. When studying the brain activity of volunteers as they were shown different brands (car manufacturers and insurers were used) and asked to answer basic attitudinal questions about them, the researchers discovered that strong brands were processed with less effort and activated areas of the brain involved in emotional processing and associated with self-identification and rewards.[36] When the impact of what's *on* the product is considered in this light, it seems optimistic, to say the least, that anything relevant to a product's sales performance would be learned from testing it "blind."

Mindful of people's capacity to fabricate answers, I tested how unreliable they can be when I worked on a brand and product development project for a biscuit manufacturer. I asked people to taste a new product (without showing them the pack) and tell me what they thought of it. There was widespread approval for the product, with a high proportion of the people interviewed claiming they would buy it if it was available where they currently bought one of the company's existing varieties. However, I was confident that launching the product would not lead to successful sales for the company. In fact it had already been on the market, stocked right next to the products the respondents had been purchasing regularly, for several years; it transpired later that several of the people I spoke to had in fact bought the product in the past. In this instance the brand's packaging didn't encourage customers to have a high regard for the taste of the product – a perception advertising had inadvertently reinforced – and, unless the brand undertook a dramatic packaging redesign, perceptions of the taste of the product wouldn't change.

Another temptation facing brand owners is to explore their brand in isolation from its product. When Lever Fabergé, part of the Unilever group, wanted to build on the success of its Lynx deodorant, it believed that research had given a clear understanding of the brand. The company was convinced that young men were attracted to the personality of the brand, rather than the brand as a deodorant.[37] It decided that Lynx could be extended into a chain of barbershops. It furnished the salons with all the things it knew appealed to young men, like gaming consoles and MTV, stocked them with Lynx products, and designed them to look "butch."[38] However, after just 14 months the project was scrapped and the salons closed; they had failed to meet their sales targets. Lever Fabergé had made the mistake of looking at just one part of the puzzle and believing what people said.

Similarly, drawing attention to an aspect of a product that seems logically relevant may well create an artificial focus on something the consumer would not consider, at least not in the way they would when forced to by an interviewer's question. When a New York liquor importer was considering importing a Swedish vodka to the US in the late 1970s, he decided to explore the potential for the product by spending over $80,000 on market research. The results were compellingly negative: people weren't interested in a Swedish vodka; some people didn't even know where Sweden was. However, the president of Carillon Importers didn't like the idea of having wasted $80,000, so decided to see if the company could sell $80,000 of vodka anyway.[39] Three decades later, over 70 million litres of Absolut are imported into the US each year.

7 Artificially reinforcing existing opinions

A few years ago I had the opportunity to watch a research agency that specialized in packaging design research moderating some focus groups for a drinks company. At the outset, the person running the group spent a large amount of time facilitating a discussion about how the respondents currently used the brand concerned. Essentially, the group conducted a mini brainstorm and eventually dredged up a large number of brand references from advertising and packaging. Among these was the shape of the bottle and the occasion on which they purchased the product.

The brand's big problem was that people only bought it once a year at Christmas. Unfortunately, the upshot of a process that forced people to appreciate that they only bought this particular product, in its particular bottle, at one time of year, was that the respondents consciously appreciated what they currently did unconsciously and therefore constructed justifications for why that would be the case. Consequently, when a series of innovative packaging designs was introduced for consideration, respondents were heavily (and unnaturally) sensitized to their existing behavior and were quick to dismiss something new; to have done so would have been to suggest that how they currently purchased the product was somehow "wrong," when they had just rehearsed with themselves and each other why it was "right." While there were numerous other reasons for this particular research approach being flawed, the fundamental problem was that the questions asked at the start of the interview had inadvertently set the tone for subsequent answers.

Most qualitative researchers conduct a "warm-up" exercise at the start of research (be it individual interviews or group discussions) to establish rapport and encourage the respondent(s) to talk openly. Unfortunately, this apparently unrelated exercise will prime people to bring particular thoughts or experiences to mind, which then color responses to subsequent questions.

Imagine that you're taking part in research and are asked: "Where did you buy your last pair of shoes?" and "Why did you buy them from the place you did?" You've just publically declared some no doubt sensible reasons for buying your shoes from wherever you bought them, a shoe shop for instance. I'm sure you could talk about your shoe purchase easily (assuming it was reasonably recent) and that, having started talking in my presence, you will feel inclined to continue doing so, even if I start to ask slightly more challenging questions. Leaving aside the previously highlighted issue that your answers will be erroneous conscious post-rationalizations of what was probably a partially unconscious experience, I've just sensitized you to a process that was almost certainly not consciously constructed in this way when it originally occurred. If I now introduce a whole new concept of shoe buying, how likely would you be to embrace it? After all, we've both just heard your very sensible reasons for using the shop you chose (and probably both for the first time, too).

8 Mistaking the value of claimed attitudes

It is relatively common for research to explore consumer attitudes to brands, products, or services. A whole raft of possible thoughts relating to a brand is devised, and research respondents are asked to say to what extent they can identify with the sentiment the statements contain; often an attitudinal scale is used so that people can indicate the degree to which they agree or disagree. There is a widespread acceptance that if you can identify someone's attitude to something then you have information that is indicative of how they will behave. Undoubtedly, this notion is attractive since it is how most people would prefer to believe they themselves function. If someone likes brand X the most, it seems logical that all things being equal, they will select brand X. Of course, things are rarely equal, and if the unconscious mind isn't filtering by likability there is no reason for the outcome to reflect that dimension.

As far back as 1934 Richard LaPiere discovered that claimed attitudes to racial prejudice didn't reflect behavior.[40] He visited more than 200 hotels and restaurants with a Chinese couple and found that only one refused to serve them. When he wrote to ask the policy of the establishment six months later, over 90% claimed they would not serve Chinese people. Subsequent studies have found virtually no correlation between attitudes and behavior across a wide range of subjects. For example, you may not be surprised to hear that a lot of people around the world have "green" attitudes but show little or no evidence of environmentally friendly behavior.[41] Similarly, we may want to believe that we like something (healthy food, for example), but an analysis of our past purchases (or waistline) may reveal that less healthy selections are made far more frequently.

In research I conducted as part of my undergraduate thesis, I explored the attitudes of 11–16-year-old schoolchildren to statistics. At the time a diverse set of subjects made some use of statistical methods and someone who ran my statistics degree course must have been interested to know whether this was destined to produce a generation of students with a passion for their subject. As part of this review I devised a questionnaire containing, among other things, a battery of attitudinal questions. The technically correct approach to such questions is to include balanced pairs statements, so that if one presents an issue negatively, another (some way down the list) will present it positively. What I discovered was that the children tended to agree with whatever statement they were answering, effectively contradicting themselves. I hypothesized at the time that they were too suggestible to use attitudinal questions reliably. I have since come to realize that several factors, not least the environment, could have contributed to this (the interviews were conducted in a school), and that the statements themselves were not likely to be a reliable indicator of anything in any case!

9 Questions inviting the wrong frame of mind

In the 1950s, Eric Berne developed a concept of how people interact, observing that the way in which they did so varied depending on the nature of the "transaction" taking place. While this is only one aspect of the psychoanalytic theory of transactional analysis that he developed – the basic "Parent–Adult–Child" model of personality (sometimes referred to as the first-order structural diagram) is the best known, the arguably more useful functional and structural variants less so – it has far-reaching implications for the accuracy of research.

What Berne realized was that there were distinct packages of thoughts, feelings, and behaviors that any one person could exhibit in response to the nature of the interpersonal exchange taking place at the time.[42] In other words, how someone is spoken to can cause them to think and behave differently.

I find that ego states – or, as I prefer to think of them, "frames of mind" – are easiest to understand through observing other people. One of the best examples I have experienced was at a Seniors Tennis event at the Royal Albert Hall. Having watched a hugely entertaining and closely contested match from very close to the action (I was seated in the front row, virtually next to a line judge), I decided on impulse to see if I could get my program signed for my young tennis-playing son by one of the most famous tennis players of all time, John McEnroe. The layout of the venue provides a great opportunity to intercept the players as they leave the auditorium: they pass through the circle seats and walk through the public corridor running around the perimeter. In my Free Child mindset I was excited and happy; I'd really enjoyed the match and wanted a token of that to share the following morning with my son, who at 4 was too young to attend the event. Just three of us waited for McEnroe to intercept him as he passed through: me, another man about my age, and a young boy, of per-haps 8 or 9 years of age. From the appearance of the others I'm sure they were as excited as me – our *thoughts*, *feelings*, and *behavior* were very much aligned, we were in the same ego state.

There was a problem, however. McEnroe had lost his match to Paul Haarhuis and he wasn't happy. He was angry, very angry. As he stomped by us the other two held out their programs. I could see trouble brewing and stood back, slipping my own program and pen behind my back. McEnroe went into a Controlling Parent mode[43] and pushed past the man, muttering angrily, a mostly "inner" voice berating himself for having lost the match. However, when he saw the child he switched briefly into a Nurturing Parent mode. He appeared happy to vent his anger at losing the match at the man, but at an unconscious level didn't want to take it out on the boy. This manifested itself as a change in muttering. I could see that McEnroe was still angry, but he was trying to accommodate the boy's request for an autograph at the same time. Presumably a Nurturing Parent frame of mind was fighting for his unconscious attention, because the person in front of him was a child.

Unfortunately, with the boy and man both still in their excited (Child) state from the entire scenario – the exciting match, the crowd, and the presence of a tennis star – they were both moving into Adapted Child, keen to accommodate the star's wishes but unable to decode what those wishes were. The result was that McEnroe attempted to indicate through his muttering that the boy follow him down the corridor and get his autograph, but that the adult go as far away as humanly possible! Because this was muttered, McEnroe still being angry at his opponent and himself, it was actually a very subtle piece of communication and only served to confuse both autograph hunters. Consequently, both followed the tennis player, who then turned on the adult and yelled at him in angry exasperation; his irritation at being pursued against his wishes became apparent.

Throw yourself into the following exercise and you'll see what I mean. Imagine that you are sitting at a desk, working, when someone comes into the room and carelessly knocks over a drink that's next to your work, ruining what you've done. How would you feel? How would you react? What would you think?

Depending on how vividly you created this scenario in your mind, you may be able to summon up a real feeling of loss, or anger, or frustration: some people report that they get a little sense of that "sick in the stomach" feeling. But the only real answer is: "It depends." There are too many variables to know what frame of mind you would be in, and you will have made a number of assumptions or ignored a number of these variables in order to arrive at your "feeling" response. Your actual frame of mind at the time it happened would determine your *actual* response.

Scenario One: You have a meeting with your boss in five minutes where you hope to secure a promotion, and it is your boss who has knocked the drink over the work.

Scenario Two: You have just solved the equations of quantum chromo-
   dynamics (don't ask me, I have no idea, it was mentioned on
   Wikipedia) and your neighbor's child, who you didn't even
   know was in the house and don't like, has chased a bouncy ball
   into the room and knocked over the beverage.

I'm guessing that your response to the two scenarios would be dramatically different. The fact is that people respond very differently
depending on the situation, their relationship with the other person
present (subservient or dominant), and their prevailing mood at the
time.

   As you will see later when I explain the AFECT criteria I
recommend for evaluating the real confidence you should have in
any consumer insight, knowing that the right frame of mind has
been involved when that insight is obtained is just as important as
asking someone who has experienced whatever you're interested in
understanding. Not only does most research ignore the variation in
frame of mind and its impact on how people fundamentally think,
feel, or behave in a particular situation, it usually creates a "transaction" to stimulate a frame of mind that suits its purposes with
total disregard for the frame of mind in operation at the consumer
moment (or moments) concerned. Market research wants *an*
answer, and in its effort to get one creates a new, unrepresentative
mindset from which the respondent replies.

   One common frame of mind elicited by consumer research[44]
is a balanced Adult ego state.

Researcher: "Please can I ask you some questions?"
Respondent: "OK."
Researcher: "Which of these brands of ice cream do you buy regularly?"

This is very considered and very rational. It seems entirely balanced, fair, and even objective. It reflects the mindset not only of
the person deconstructing the marketing issue to devise the questions the company wants answering, but also of the people who
will hear the answers and consider what the company should do
as a result. But what if you sometimes buy ice cream to eat because

you feel sad, because your Child ego state needs cheering up? Eric Berne observed three distinct packages of thoughts, feelings, and behaviors. Which "package" is the respondent asked about ice cream going to call to mind? The process of research has done its best to ensure that they aren't thinking or feeling in a Child frame of mind and the process of artificial post-rationalization has been further encouraged. Asking someone in a different frame of mind is like asking a different person.

Focus groups tend to have more variation in their encouragement of respondent ego state. Sometimes they invite the balanced (Adult) consideration that emanates from specifically inviting a group of people to a place and paying them to think about something and talk about it.

There is a very effective technique that Thomas Harris describes called "Parent Shrinking," which can be used to shift people who are being belligerent and inflexible about a particular issue to a more balanced frame of mind; in other words, that will move them from Parent to Adult.[45] Essentially, all it involves is remaining calm and balanced oneself and asking genuine questions. For example:

Person one (angrily): "I can't believe you'd be so stupid as leave your coat at home today!"

Person two (calmly): "Why are you concerned about me and my coat?"

Person one (still angrily): "You're going to catch your death of cold, you idiot."

Person two (still calmly): "Are you worried that I might get ill?"

Person one (calming down): "Errr, yes, I don't want you to be ill, it will spoil our holiday next week if you are."

Person two: "I feel OK, actually, but perhaps we shouldn't stay out too long."

Person one: "OK, and let's walk more quickly so you stay warm."

This may sound a little contrived. In practice, it is actually very difficult to "break" the transaction that another person initiates[46] because, before you've consciously shifted your position, you've been unconsciously primed either to be belligerent back (a Parent response such as "You're not my mother, I'm perfectly capable of deciding what to wear") or to respond deferentially (a Child response such as a sulky tut followed by an unconvincing "Sorry").

If you consider an exchange during a consumer research depth interview or focus group where a respondent becomes angry about a brand or experience, you'll appreciate the typical nature of this type of transaction. Research moderators and interviewers are trained to be dispassionate and balanced; after all, they are interested in understanding what the person thinks, and are not taking it as a personal attack. How do they react? They ask balanced questions, ostensibly to understand why the respondent feels so angry. The psychological consequence of this is that the respondent's anger dissipates and they may well start opining a more balanced and reasonable position than the one they would otherwise hold and that they would "naturally" access in a real-life experience with the brand concerned. Which point in this transition will the researcher report?

Derren Brown recounts a more extreme form of this technique in his book *Tricks of the Mind*. When affronted by an aggressive and provocative drunk man late one evening, Brown describes derailing the potential attack using confusion. He said something to the man, in a calm and balanced (Adult) tone, that was completely unrelated to the aggressor's line of thinking. The mental change of direction was sufficient to derail the train of thought of the person looking for a fight and shift the balance of power. Brown survived unscathed, bar the pain of a drunken chap recounting his unhappy night out.

I have seen consumer research group moderators deploy the same technique when they "move on" with an unrelated question from their list to stem the tide of a respondent's critical outburst. In gaining control of the respondent's frame of mind they may move further away from their true mental frame of reference. Ultimately, a reasoned response, while most pleasant to hear and potentially attractive to the audience for the research, isn't necessarily accurate.

In the case of the Millennium Dome, an inherently rational interview process, comprising a number of questions, was evaluating what most people would approach as a "playful" day out. In posing the rational suggestion "Are you going to commemorate this historic moment by attending the main event this country is laying on to celebrate it?", it is not surprising that so many people thought they might go along. However, had the organizers attached more weight to the number of people who *actually* make the effort to travel any distance to attend a themed event (such as a theme park or historic building) in any given year, they might have recognized that they were going to need to create something monumentally thrilling to cause six times that number of people to change their behavior and embrace the Dome as a new alternative.[47]

It's essential to consider what frame of mind a person is likely to be in when they are really engaged in whatever the research has raised with them, and if they would even be mindful of it at all. If the frame of mind induced by the research is different, the response probably will be too.

10 Another "how we think" problem

The way in which people think about something is a by-product of the experiences they've had up to that point and how easy or difficult it is to think about. Unfortunately, it's often extremely difficult to know which experiences someone will mentally associate with a question and how easy or hard they are finding it. However, depending on what associations they make, their responses can differ dramatically.

This was highlighted by a study that asked people to assess their risk of heart disease in the context of behaviors that either increased or decreased their likelihood of getting the condition. When participants without any history of heart disease in their family were asked to think of eight risk-increasing behaviors, the difficulty they had thinking of so many caused them to rate their own vulnerability *lower* than when they were asked to think of just three, and lower than when they had been asked to think of three or eight risk-lowering behaviors.[48] When those asked were people *with* a family history of heart disease, who could be expected to think about the question more deeply as a result, the results were completely different. They perceived their risk as being higher when they thought about eight risk-*increasing* behaviours or three risk-*decreasing* behaviors.

Other studies have found that changing how a statement is presented, in terms of how easy or difficult it is to read on the page, influences the extent to which people believe it or not. Where people struggle with a question, or can't be bothered to think about it, they will answer differently from when the question or the answer is easier to access.

In the research conducted for the Millennium Dome, potential visitors were classified as "persuadables" if they agreed with statements such as "I will decide nearer the time (if I'm going to visit the Dome)." All the potential mental complexity of deciding about a group trip to Greenwich and paying to visit a somewhat esoterically defined attraction could be neatly deferred by agreeing to "think about it."

11 The peril of being nice when asking questions

Frequently, a researcher's training to "facilitate" a discussion will covertly encourage a particular type of response. If you have ever viewed a focus group, you may have noticed that very often the moderator will lean forward, sitting with very "open" body language, and look up slightly at the people seated in the horseshoe-arranged chairs. The moderator's voice will be quite bright and bouncy. This is an understandable package of behaviors for the moderator to adopt: the purpose is to initiate a discussion on a particular subject and the open posture and bouncy tone say "I'm receptive; this is nice; talk to me."

Unfortunately, this package of behavior has been observed to encourage a particular response. Work by clinical psychologist Kahler identified a number of packages of behaviors as a tool for assessing personality.[49] One of them includes the following traits:

- ◆ "Bouncy" high... but low... speech. Using expressions like "OK?," All right," and "Hmmm?."
- ◆ A high tone of voice that rises at the end of a sentence.
- ◆ Frequent head nodding, with hands reaching out and palms up
- ◆ Leaning forward toward the other person (or people) and nodding the head.
- ◆ Looks up under raised eyebrows, exaggerated smiles with teeth bared.

The list, which in my experience could just as easily be a training manual for focus group moderators, is classified as the "Please You" behavior driver. As the name suggests, the "return" on adopting this pattern of behavior is a greater chance of the recipient(s) liking you. This is understandable from the perspective of getting a group of strangers to start talking, but highly dubious if the intention is to have them be totally authentic. The problem for research is that using this driver has been shown to invite a similar response: the respondent likes the researcher and is inclined to say things that they believe will please them.

At a fundamental level, the moderator is saying: "Look how nice, unthreatening, and approachable I am." The response it typically elicits is: "I'll be nice too." This is hardly a recipe for discovering fundamental consumer truths. I can only speculate what proportion of new product concepts have flown with flying colors through an evaluation process in focus groups because the moderator made everyone a little *too* at ease with him or her.

12 Imagine you're a helicopter...

Another frame-of-mind distortion practiced in research comes from so-called projective techniques. For the uninitiated, this term covers a range of questioning techniques originally developed by psychologists that are designed to encourage respondents to go past the obvious and/or limited ways in which they might describe something, a brand for instance, and talk about it indirectly. Because respondents are presented with an ambiguous stimulus to respond to, their choice of response is presumed to reveal something of their underlying thoughts about it.

While opinions about the efficacy of projective techniques vary among psychologists, the main problem with their use in consumer research is the frame of mind they invoke in respondents. Consider the following request:

> "I'd like you to pretend that this brand is a person. What would the person be like? What might they wear? What sort of car would they drive? Where would they live?" (I won't go on, but you get the idea.)

People will typically react in one of two ways: either they will glaze over and not "get" the concept at all, or they will play the game and start providing answers. However, what they're doing in transactional analysis terms is going into a Child ego state; they get over the fact that they feel silly and get into what's being asked of them. This raises the question of whether their usual interaction with the brand is from a Child ego state. If it is, then the thoughts, feelings, and behaviors they tap into in connection with the brand and the projective exercise *may* be an accurate reflection of those associated with moments of consumption. If not, then however well intentioned, the answers they provide are probably not an indication of their real thoughts and feelings. Not for the first time, I would argue, the convenience of a technique that can be very good at providing research data – very good in the sense of the volume produced and how interesting it seems – has little to offer by way of dependable accuracy.

Creative questioning styles can provide more interesting responses, but they are not necessarily more reliable. If any of the research techniques used has induced a frame of mind that is not present during the actual consumer experience, it is unlikely to have obtained an accurate picture of what people think.

13 Your customers can't be trusted

It might seem sensible for organizations seeking to understand what they're doing well or what they should do next to ask their current customers to evaluate their products or services. When the results come back, who could blame them for supposing that such ratings provide a representative indication of how they are perceived or what people want? However, even once all the potential distortions of the research process discussed to this point have been taken into consideration, another issue exists: people who have gone to the trouble of purchasing something tend to value it more highly than people who haven't.

This was one of the reasons I was able to predict accurately that the advice I gave some friends on what new car to buy would be ignored. They called to ask my opinion, as they were considering replacing their large car for something more practical and took my interest in the motoring section of their Sunday paper as an indication of expertise. I listened to their needs, did some research, and told them which model would, in my opinion, be best. Unfortunately, another couple who were friends of theirs had recently purchased a car different from the one I was advocating and had enthused to them about it. I suspected, rightly as it turned out, that my balanced appraisal would stand little chance against the post-purchase-endowed priming from their friends.

This phenomenon, known as the "endowment effect," was first identified by Richard Thaler in 1980. As the experiment with the coffee mug in the previous chapter revealed, it only takes a few moments of ownership for people to value something significantly more highly. Another study, conducted in the late 1990s, highlighted just how powerful this effect can be. Obtaining tickets to a popular basketball game at Duke University was a major challenge: people had to overcome queues *and* win in a raffle to secure a ticket. Researchers asked people who had managed to buy a ticket what they would be prepared to sell it for, and compared this with the amount people who hadn't managed to get one would be willing to pay. The difference was dramatic: people who had won a ticket valued it, on average, at $2,411; those who hadn't won valued it at just $166.[50] When it comes to ascertaining how much you can sell something for, the only reliable test is to try to sell it at a particular price and see what happens.

In its report on the Millennium Dome, the UK National Audit Office was quick to report the good news: the second point in its executive summary was that "87% of visitors were satisfied with their visit."[51] Leaving aside the somewhat abstract nature of the word "satisfied," how should one interpret this statistic? Does it mean that the Dome experience was actually good and that the marketing agencies are to blame for the poor number of visitors? Does it imply that the critics were wrong in suggesting that it wasn't very good? Or is it simply a reflection of the fact that, once they've paid for and experienced something, people may rate it far more highly than others who haven't?

How wrong can research be?

Any one of the 13 issues I've described can cause misleading research results, but when they work in combination with each other the impact can be extraordinary. Typically, the process of asking consumers what they think is either a one-off exercise or else repeated in a consistent fashion, resulting in no point of comparison, merely a consistent error that goes unnoticed. However, opinion polls are occasionally conducted with genuine independence, allowing us to see the potential range of outcomes created by compounding some of these question issues.

On September 10, 2009, an article entitled "Cut the TV Licence Fee by £5.50, Says the BBC Chairman" was published in the *Daily Telegraph*.[52] The background to this issue is that a small proportion of the money collected from the £142.50 license for watching television has been used to help elderly and disabled people make the move over to digital television; once this switch has been completed the government is planning to use this money to fund local news on commercial channels. The article explained that an opinion poll conducted for the BBC Trust had found that "only 6 per cent of more than 2000 people surveyed for the Trust by

Ipsos MORI supported the idea of using the surplus to help other broadcasters."

This would appear to be a convincing argument for the government reconsidering its intentions, until you look at the questions they asked more closely and discover that in the course of the interviews three clear errors were made:[53]

◆ Respondents were primed with information they wouldn't normally be cognizant of regarding the level of the license fee and the fact that a proportion was being used to subsidize digital switchover.
◆ The questionnaire forced certainty by not explicitly allowing people to say that they weren't sure about the issue.
◆ Of the six alternative uses for the money offered for consideration, only one was concrete (reducing the level of the license fee by £5.50), the remaining five were abstract ("Helping to increase...", "Funding..." and "Spending more..."). Who could say what difference these might make to anyone's life?

It's also worth observing that while it is true that from the questionnaire used only 6% of respondents selected the option proposed by the government – funding other news programs – less than half of those interviewed said that they wanted to see the license fee reduced and 51% of people selected one of the five abstract options as their preference.

One week later, the *Daily Telegraph* published another article on the subject under the headline: "Most voters want BBC to share the licence fee."[54] This time it was reporting the UK government's own 2,000-person survey of opinions conducted by TNS-BMRB on what people thought should happen to the license fee money that was becoming available. This time the polling company did at least check whether or not it was priming respondents with new information: apparently 71% of them weren't aware that they had been funding the switch to digital television for the elderly and disabled. However, an appreciation that, through the interview process, the company was artificially informing the respondents didn't stop it carrying on with the questions and publishing its results.[55]

According to the newspaper article, "Two thirds of those surveyed... said a proportion of the licence fee should be used to support regional news on other channels such as ITV." One reason for the dramatic difference in results is that respondents weren't given the option of having the money deducted from the license fee.

When the question was asked initially, 48% thought that the money should be used to support channels other than the BBC. Later, after a series of questions asking about the frequency they "watch/listen to/look at" national and regional news, the importance of having news provided by more than one source, and a statement explaining that the primary commercial channel, ITV, had said it may "no longer be able to afford to provide regional or local news," a proportion of two thirds was achieved. Again, while the polling company did ask if respondents were aware of ITV's statement about withdrawing its local news coverage, and learned that three quarters were not and had therefore been artificially primed by the poll itself, it didn't prevent the government from publishing the results and, presumably, using them to inform its own decision making. Nor did it stop the polling company's author stating in the report's introduction that the questionnaire had been tested through a "cognitive pilot" so that "the questions would deliver an accurate and unbiased measure of public opinion."[56]

So which poll is a correct gauge of public opinion? Neither. Rather, they both demonstrate perfectly how the process of inviting responses in research produces answers that are a by-product of the questioning process. Even if a standardized approach to such research could be agreed on, it would still be inherently flawed. The research process creates a focus that ordinarily doesn't exist and wraps a frame around it that can't help but shape the outcome.

Learning to ignore the irrelevant consumer

The desire to solicit consumer opinion through questions is evidently a compelling one. Examples abound of contradictory poll results, inaccurate election forecasts, and feedback that appears to bear no relation to corresponding sales data. And yet the presentation of customer data as support or evidence in political argument and corporate decision making is perpetuated. The problem is a result of the human mind's disposition for confirmation bias. I would go so far as to suggest that virtually everyone who regularly uses consumer research data has, on occasion, opted to ignore it or else dismissed it as wrong. As with any belief or superstition, people have no problem selectively discounting those occasions when they've become temporarily "research agnostic" and continue to behave in keeping with the belief that gives them comfort.

Our brains are highly adept at spotting patterns of cause and effect, but that means that we frequently misattribute chance events as having some underlying reason.[57] When the data supports a decision that turns out well, that's perceived as evidence that asking consumers questions is inherently worthwhile; when the findings from research are found wanting, they are soon forgotten. We need to acknowledge that, most of the time, we expect far too much from people in anticipating that they will be able to account for themselves and their opinions through a question-and-answer process that influences their thinking in such a way that it stops them from being the consumer we seek to understand.

These dynamic aspects of personality are largely ignored by consumer research. It prefers instead to subscribe to a constant or "average" theory of personality: people will do more or less what they do wherever they are and whatever else is going on. In fact, what people do and how they do it is not a given. They operate on the basis of cause-and-effect contingencies that are dependent both on the prevailing events at the time and on how the events are unconsciously processed and consciously interpreted.[58]

You might very well ask what one can reasonably ask and how one should ask it. This is a question that, commissioning influences aside, polling companies have been battling with since the 1930s. It is entirely reasonable to ask whether an answer, in terms of finding a valid opinion polling approach, exists at all. Is the constant fascination with soliciting opinions simply a by-product of our own conscious delusions? We would like to believe that we know what we think and therefore it seems reasonable that others will know their own minds.

So are there *any* questions worth asking? And if so, when and how should we ask them?

6

RELEVANT ANSWERS

Questions worth asking

As I explained in the preceding chapters, the fact that people *can* post-rationalize their behavior, or will answer a question on the basis of what they believe they think, doesn't mean that they do so accurately in terms of the way they will subsequently behave. Beyond that, taking a person out of the environment in which they make judgments about consumption creates an even greater risk that, however well intentioned they are, their responses won't reflect how they will think and act when those influences are present. As I discussed in the last chapter, these problems are compounded when the process of questioning alters what people think and say.

Most research is preoccupied with getting people to answer: to say something, anything, that can be analyzed. The barometer of validity that tends to be applied is whether the same response is heard consistently. This may very well indicate nothing more than that people respond in the same way because the *process* of research was more or less the same, rather than because the repeated responses reflect some underlying truth.

The time and place

The best time for asking questions is when the behavior of the person being questioned has been observed. That way, any claims made can at least be compared and contrasted with what was seen and, to an extent, validated accordingly. The best place to ask a question is when the respondent is as close as possible to the environmental and contextual elements that influenced their behavior;

unlike with research conducted in any other location, the only additional sources of inadvertent influence are then the questions and the person asking them.

It is also advantageous to be asking the questions relatively soon after the consumer choice or experience has taken place. Given our capacity for consciously rationalizing a nonconflicting, positively embellished perspective of the things we've found ourselves doing, the longer we have to construct an apparently sensible rationale for our actions, the greater the likelihood that we will do so.

When considering emotional responses, such as how someone feels about a brand or an advertisement, there is a strong argument for only paying significant attention to their instantaneous reaction. The longer people have to involve their conscious mind, the more likely they will be to adapt that reaction to one that is influenced by social factors that would ordinarily not be involved, such as who else is present and how they would like to be perceived by other people. Think of it as the difference between that moment when someone makes a tremendous belch and is really quite pleased with the sound they've produced, and the moment they remember they should be embarrassed at something generally considered socially unacceptable.

A number of studies have shown that our unconscious mind's response occurs some time before we reach a conscious conclusion about something. In addition to the decks of cards experiment mentioned in Chapter 1, Benjamin Libet and his colleagues scrutinized the brain and muscle activity of people asked to tap their finger at random and discovered that the conscious experience to move the finger happened a third of a second *after* the activity in the brain that initiated it.[1] More recently, researchers in Berlin found that brain activity preceded the conscious awareness of selecting one of two buttons by as much as seven seconds.[2]

More evidence of the important link between speed of response and the unconscious mind can be found in the Implicit Association Test, developed by Greenwald, Banaji, and Nosek. It was devised to reveal the underlying unconscious associations that influence our beliefs and behavior and does so by asking participants to categorize words as quickly as possible and comparing reaction times; where the response is quicker the unconscious association is stronger.[3]

Of course, with traditional approaches to soliciting consumer views, the efficacy is associated with the depth of probing and the cost of the research is closely linked to the length of interview or discussion. But with the perils of introspection and post-rationalization, ironically the mechanism through which value and quality is implicitly judged is indicative of a barrier to accuracy.

In a nutshell, the longer the pause between the question and the response, the greater the likelihood that the conscious mind has intervened and wielded its duplicitous influence on what's going to follow.

Asking the right mindset

A lot of research sampling and recruitment screening concerns itself with asking the right person, but how do you ensure that you are then asking the right *mindset* of that person, and how do you do this if you can't catch them just after the moment of interest?

Fortunately, while it's impossible to force someone to shift into a different mindset against their will, it's surprisingly easy to encourage them to do so. If you think about an emotional experience you've had in the past – a powerfully unhappy one will perhaps help make the point best – you may look back on it with a degree of sadness. As you reflect, you know that it was a sad event but you are anesthetized from it by the passage of time. Your unconscious mind has done its job in assimilating the feeling and returning you to the same level of happiness you were always at.[4] However, if you start to recall what you did at the time – in other words, the behavioral experiences you had – the feelings you experienced start to return; perhaps not as powerfully as they did originally, but your basic frame of mind will shift to the one you occupied then and the emotions you experienced will return.

Even if you can't take yourself into this mental state, you can easily observe the process in interviews with people who have had traumatic experiences. Recently I watched two documentaries about people who had been directly or indirectly caught up in the terrorist attacks on London in July 2005. As they relived their experiences of that day for the journalist, their emotional state shifted to the one they had occupied at the time. The wife who couldn't get hold of her husband started to cry again; Susanna Pell, an extraordinary woman who had found the composure and bravery to walk into the bombed carriage and save lives, exhibited the resolve and calmness she had discovered in herself that day. In both of these cases the people concerned had no desire, derived no benefit, and made no conscious attempt to shift back into that mindset, it happened unconsciously.

These extreme cases reveal that people can be reversed into an unconscious mindset by a questioning process that causes them to reflect on their behavior, rather than post-rationalize it. In my experience this technique doesn't only work with experiences involving significant emotions; people will also shift their frame of mind to relive more mundane experiences, particularly when they are relatively recent.

In his book *The Feeling of What Happens*, one of the world's leading experts on neurophysiology, Antonio Damasio, reveals why emotions are so critical to how we process information:

> In a typical emotion, then, certain regions of the brain, which are part of a largely preset neural system related to emotions, send commands to other regions of the brain and to most everywhere in the body proper. One route is the bloodstream, where the commands are sent in the form of chemical molecules that act on the receptors in the cells which constitute body tissues. The other route consists of neuron pathways and the commands along this route take the form of electrochemical signals which act on other neurons or on muscular fibers or on organs (such as the adrenal gland) which in turn can release chemicals of their own into the bloodstream.[5]

If the process reveals the mindset that a consumer was in at the time of interest, it is then possible, with an understanding of how Eric Berne's transactional states interact with one another, to talk to respondents in a way that encourages them to stay in the frame of mind concerned and elicit further information about what they were thinking and feeling. When combined with observation of actual behavior, this approach provides a combination of factual evidence and psychoanalysis that can be particularly informative.

Word scrutiny

I have explored countless reasons why it is reckless and misleading for consumer research to work on the principle that consumers can tell us what they think and feel. I find it is invariably better to design investigations into consumers' thoughts, feelings, and behaviors on the basis that they *can't* tell us what they think. Whenever it becomes helpful or necessary to question consumers, it is essential that what they say is treated with enormous skepticism.

One way of assessing the accuracy of a response is to pay close attention to the language the person is using. Psychoanalysts are wary of people who say they will "try" to do something; as commitments go it's not exactly a powerful statement of intent. Similarly, when respondents are talking about their attitude to a brand, product, service, or piece of marketing communication, their words may reveal that they are being socially considerate rather than entirely honest. When people drop pronouns such as "I" and "we" in association with an opinion, it suggests a personal affinity with what follows. In contrast, when they unconsciously distance themselves from a statement by saying something like "It's nice" rather than "I like it," there are grounds to be suspicious.[6]

It is also helpful to look for correlations between people's behavior and their claimed attitudes or values. It's easy for us all to make claims (based on the not-always-unhealthy mechanism of self-delusion) that we are striving for something positive when there may be significant clues that suggest we aren't quite attaining the values to which we aspire. If someone sets out to tell a lie, then it takes a reasonable amount of practice and skill to establish a base line and detect the micro facial reactions, verbal pauses, and stress cues that can indicate an attempt at deception. However, when people are lying to themselves it is generally easier to identify. Indeed, the main challenge is lifting ourselves above the acquired level of social interaction that leads us, by and large, to accept what other people tell us is true, particularly if it's relayed in a compelling way. It does feel as though you are doubting the person concerned (naturally enough, because you are) and is not necessarily going to result in an exchange that endears you to the other person; although in my experience people aren't usually hostile when, through the process of asking the right questions, they realize that they have been misleading themselves too.

For example, in a project testing advertising, someone dismissed an ad and claimed that he wanted a more factual and informative advert from the company concerned. By distracting him with an irrelevant topic for a moment (so that he didn't see the association) and then quickly asking him to state what his favorite advert was, I established that that ad was in no way factual or informative. Evidently he didn't like the ad I had shown him, but had I advised my client that it should produce an infomercial based on comments like this one, I would have been doing the client a huge disservice.

Sometimes it's not even necessary to ask a question. When someone says that they have been buying a product for years because they're on a diet, the statement seems reasonable enough. But when that person is significantly overweight, it is apparent that, unless they started out at a size that would have made the national news, they aren't shedding pounds at any discernable rate; it is likely that they are actually buying the product for another reason altogether.

Another way in which people's conscious misinterpretations can be manifested is when they are inconsistent with other behaviors. For example, in one project looking at supermarket shopping, I spoke to several women who, despite taking the time to write a shopping list, routinely forgot to take it with them. They rationalized this as trivial forgetfulness rather than anything more duplicitous, but when I asked them how many times they forgot to take their money or to put clothes on, the answer was never. I deduced that there must be an unconscious basis for forgetting the lists and, by exploring their behavior on shopping trips, could start to explore why this really happened.

Another technique for getting behind the conscious veil people like to keep in front of themselves, particularly where you suspect that they are putting on a show for your benefit, is to switch the focus of the conversation from them to "other people." On the basis that what people see in others reflects their own perspective, asking consumers what they think other people's motives are can be enlightening. Customers who are unwilling to reveal their own confusion with a product display will often be happy to point out that "other people" would find it confusing. One word of warning though: it's important to distinguish those responses that are the result of you having asked the respondent to represent the views of others from when they voluntarily do so. The latter can be a form of social politeness, for example when they think something is hopeless but they try to soften the blow by suggesting that someone else (who isn't present) would think it was terrific.

Asking indirectly related questions can also help distinguish genuine motivations from positions adopted to be socially acceptable. Few people would admit that they choose a brand for reasons of elitism or snobbery, but, where you suspect this is the case, asking them if they would describe users of the brand as more successful or more intelligent than nonusers can be revealing. It's important to play close attention to the total package of the response to such questions. In one case where I used this approach the woman replied "I wouldn't say that," while shifting her position into a more upright and assured pose, and placing a little more emphasis on the word "that." She wouldn't necessarily *say* that she was better than people who didn't use the brand, but her reaction suggested that she was happy to think it.

In a project for a vegetarian food product, one pack design was being rejected out of hand by a subgroup of the target audience and favored by the others. There was something distinctive about the type of people involved, though: their behavior and style of dress suggested that they saw themselves as set apart from the others. Through asking them questions that were about other aspects of their lifestyle, it emerged that their vegetarianism was a reflection of a greater stance against mainstream culture and, as a result, they didn't like the pack design *because* it made the product more commercially attractive. Being commercially attractive was exactly what my client wanted, and with the evidence I obtained the company could at least make an informed decision about what proportion of its existing customers it risked losing by changing to a pack that had the potential to appeal far more widely.

Taking a skeptical position on consumer post-rationalizations is eminently sensible. Recently, a client of mine described research he'd conducted suggesting that people leaving his company's stores without purchasing were doing so because the store didn't have the specific product they wanted. This simple and eminently reasonable explanation, captured from interviews with customers as they left the store, could easily have been accepted at face value. However, my client has a healthy skepticism when it comes to consumer research and commissioned a further study to ask people *entering* the store what they had come to buy. It transpired that most customers didn't have a specific product in mind. It's much easier to tell yourself that you haven't bought something because the shop didn't have what you wanted than it is to appreciate that the store environment didn't make you want to spend longer, the salesperson failed to influence you in the right way, the product display confused you too much to be able to make a choice, or you were scared you'd buy the wrong thing (all much more likely reasons for not parting with your money).

Ask leading questions

For understandable reasons, most people who come into contact with market research regard leading questions as a potential source of bias rather than a tool for getting an accurate insight into the consumer mind. However, in the right context, leading questions have the capacity to provide more powerful and more accurate insights than balanced ones.

When behavioral evidence has been collected, even if it's at a market level rather than for the individual concerned, building this knowledge into questions can have the effect of giving the respondent tacit permission to say something that they otherwise wouldn't. For example, if the behavioral evidence shows that most people walk around part of a store looking confused, it can be much more effective to say to people "Most customers find this part of the store really confusing, why do you think that is?", rather than to allow conscious vanity to present the respondent as a rare example of someone who could cope with the experience. In any event, if they haven't experienced the problem their answer will tend to reflect this.

Similarly, rather than using a totally dispassionate and balanced style of questioning, it can be beneficial to adopt a position that reflects behavior. When interviewing people about financial services products, I have often found it more helpful to be empathetically confused about product details, rather than allow the respondent to feel stupid on their own because they don't understand the technicalities of a product they will only encounter once or twice in their lives.

Confirmation and clarification

One of the most helpful uses of questions is to confirm and clarify what has been observed at a behavioral level. Very often this involves confirming what you believe consumers *haven't* taken any notice of. For example, it is much more useful to put a piece of point-of-sale communication advertising – say, the availability of next-day delivery – into the environment in which it will have to operate and ask: "How soon could you get that delivered if you wanted it?" If people say "Tomorrow", ask if that information is provided anywhere in the store. You will recall from the phenomenon of inattentional blindness that people are perfectly capable of not seeing something that they have looked at. From my own work I know that people can select from a list of a dozen television programs, having looked at the list for over ten seconds, and be incapable of recalling any program other than the one they selected once the list has been removed. One of the ways I confirm this is by challenging people to name what's on a given channel to win £100. Not only can they not do it, but on occasions they will claim that a program guide from which they have chosen thousands of times doesn't have information about the channel each program is on, despite its always having been there.

Conversely, just because something hasn't been consciously noticed doesn't mean that it hasn't influenced a consumer. Issues surrounding quality of finish of the materials used in the environment, packaging design, and the nature of surrounding products can all influence consumers' unconscious perceptions. This is why having the true behavioral measure of observed consumer activity is so important, and is where having a carefully constructed test-and-control methodology can be revealing.

When the subject of such tests needs to be explicitly processed, such as with specific promotional messages, clarifying awareness in the way I have described is worthwhile. However, questioning can also be useful to support tested elements that one would expect to be processed predominantly at an unconscious level. Here, the challenge is to identify the correlated factors and compare them in test-and-control conditions. For example, people's assessments about the size of a range may be inversely proportional to the actual range if an aspect of the fixture enables them to appreciate more of the products available when there is more space between them. Asking them how many products they thought were available shortly after they've left that part of the store can confirm that one display is working better than another in this regard.

It is possible to identify confirmatory questions for many of the factors that influence the unconscious mind:

♦ Establishing that someone has bought the same product that they did previously is a clue that risk aversion may have driven choice. For purchases that aren't routine, if people only have a point of justification for the product they have bought, as opposed to a comparative measure with an understanding of the data for the competitor they rejected, the chances are that they have played it safe.

♦ Asking where else they have seen a product or who else they know who owns it can help identify where social proof has played a part.

♦ Understanding the amount of attention paid to competing products can indicate how unconsciously "fluent" the purchase is. When I watch people walk straight up to a product and take it without following the action of their hand and arm, I can be fairly sure that the customer is sufficiently comfortable with their choice to leave the physical act of taking it to their unconscious mind. When I ask people who have shopped in this way what competing products were available, they often can't name any at all.

♦ Identifying how someone references a purchase in relation to other products can indicate where frames and extremeness aversion have been influential.

♦ Asking someone what other (unrelated) products the shop sells can highlight (through the order in which they're accessed and the nature of those products) how the customer perceives the purchase more broadly, and may indicate whether other products have contributed to the unconscious perception of the one selected. A retail client asked me to explore the appeal of a competitor which was always mentioned in glowing terms by its customers. Among many factors I identified, it was apparent that people referenced the premium brands of the competitor and, despite the fact that those same brands were available at both stores, the unknown brands that my client pushed to the fore because they were relatively inexpensive. As a result of this frame of reference, all the products in my client's store seemed less attractive.

Contradictions

Some of the most powerful insights occur where questioning reveals a contradiction between behavior, attitudes, and experience. For example, one friend of mine is almost evangelical about the Apple brand and, following his purchase of an iPod a couple of years ago, has rapidly bought desktop and laptop computers, an iPod shuffle, and an iPhone. He is swift to tell me that, whatever gadget I may be considering, I should get an Apple version if it exists. Recently, I watched as a colleague of his asked him for advice on which laptop to buy. Sure enough, he recommended an Apple product, and regaled the person with an explanation of how they were immune to viruses and how stable the operating system was. Shortly afterwards, I was with the same friend when, to his evident irritation, his iPhone locked up. It transpired that this had happened several times over recent weeks. This unwillingness to attribute the problems he was having with one product to the brand as a whole are a powerful indication of his relationship with the brand and reflect the bias that we all tend to exhibit (except when we're forced to be artificially rational by consumer research).

When observing consumers in retail environments, I often find that their behavior isn't congruent with what they tell me. A customer may justify their choice as being "the best product" for them, but if they haven't done research prior to visiting the store and haven't spent an adequate amount of time looking at the alternatives available, it is an indication that they have a deeper relationship with the brand they've chosen than its competitors. The right probing usually reveals what form this relationship takes and how it has influenced their behavior.

The accuracy of a customer's critical assessment of their experience, in comparison with what has been observed, is also usually enlightening. Since for the most part our minds work to select the evidence that reinforces our initial perceptions, what customers allow themselves to notice reveals a great deal about what they feel about the product, brand, or retailer concerned.

Summarizing the lessons from the Dome

There is still a place for asking consumers questions, but that place isn't anywhere near the start of the process of understanding consumers and it should never involve taking what people say at face value. The fundamental nature of the interview must be totally shifted. When the unconscious mind is involved in consumer behavior – and it always is – it is futile to believe that respondents can accurately supply the information required to guide commercial decisions. Instead, the *right* questions can help substantiate or expand on what has been observed. It is essential to start with the principle that consumers *can't* tell you what they think, not that they *will*.

In my experience, people answering market researchers' questions aren't usually actively attempting to deceive anyone (including themselves). When a respondent says "I didn't realize I did that, but I do," it's a good indication that you've reached a point of insight into the workings of their unconscious mind.

Respondents are, unfortunately, far too willing to answer questions. One can only wonder about the spectacular event imagined by the respondents who said they were likely to go to visit the Millennium Dome. What is clear is that they were happy to imagine and speculate when the only logical response would have been to say: "How the heck should I know if I'll go to this event that hasn't been conceived yet?"

In cases where the only route to reassurance about a future consumer-directed initiative is through an artificial research process (as opposed to a live trial), by taking care to replicate the likely frame of mind and contextual influences, and by being mindful of the potential biases and influences inherent in the research process, it is possible to reduce the risk of getting a misleading reading. In this sense, a convenient approach can be made more reliable than most current approaches manage to be.

Careful consideration needs to be given to the sequencing of questions in research. It is foolhardy to discount the unconscious sensitization and associations formed in a respondent's mind by one question or comment prior to another – be it what is asked of them or what they hear themselves say in reply. There is much to be said for the one-question survey.

If the subject of research is to do with the present – current attitudes or feelings, for example – the process must start with questions that focus on behavior rather than post-rationalized thoughts and feelings. It is imperative that a respondent isn't aware of the subject of the research, which makes it much more difficult for them to filter and frame their responses. People frequently think about *why* they do things, justifying that to themselves and others, but far less about *what* they have done. This not only provides a basis against which to judge the congruence of subsequently expressed attitudes and feelings, it also helps move the frame of mind from one conditioned by the research process to one in line with the consumer experience of interest.

Following this, I advocate asking questions to explore what elements of unconscious influence might have motivated the behavior. Again, this gives priority to the role of the unconscious over the conscious constructions that may have been made after the event to support consumers' view of themselves as autonomous, consciously driven, independent beings. Subsequent questioning *can* invite the respondent's post-rationalizations and conscious analysis, because by this stage there is a base against which to judge its congruence.

Had the Dome research discovered that respondents' previous visits to theme-park-style attractions had been infrequent and spontaneous decisions, the researchers might have been less tempted to suppose that their own attraction would draw so many people. If they had doubted the veracity of the research process, they might have asked the same people how many were likely to visit an existing attraction and, when the real numbers of visitors were available, concluded that theme-park visitors weren't reliable predictors of their own behavior. Nevertheless, with the added complexities of its not being an established attraction and the likely consequence of priming respondents to contemplate an event laden with contextual excitement (essentially the researchers were asking: "Are you going to celebrate the year 2000 by going to the Millennium Dome or can you think of something better?"), the results would still have been misleading.

In many ways, when it comes to asking people questions to inform decisions, it is a case of recognizing the involvement of the unconscious mind and digging around for clues about how it has been influenced. Equally, an acute understanding of the way in which this part of our mind, to which we have no direct access, drives our behavior generally can help identify the likely challenges that any new initiative will have to overcome. Against that background, there is another aspect of human behavior that is far more influential than most of us are willing to concede. To be successful any organization must connect with it but, paradoxically, never ask for its perspective. We must understand the crowd.

7

UNDERSTANDING THE CROWD

Focusing on focus groups

Just as we are unaware of how our physical environment influences our thoughts and behavior, we don't appreciate the subtle but significant influence that the actions of other people can have on us. Cults, religions, and brands all rely on some aspect of group influence to spread their message, sometimes with astonishing speed.

History is littered with examples of times when groups have been influenced to behave in a way that can seem incomprehensible to others. When it came to power, the Nazi Party had two million members; by the time of its demise, it had more than eight million.[1] While many of these people joined for career reasons, it has been estimated that there was an active membership of at least one million people, many of whom were in senior positions in the national government and to a greater or lesser degree integral to its nefarious objectives. In 1933, 44% of the German electorate voted for Hitler's party. No doubt most of us would like to believe that we wouldn't have been persuaded by the rhetoric of the day, but the reality is that it's not just what is said that matters: the number of people around you who are nodding their heads can change what you think.

Shaping what the crowd thinks doesn't necessarily require a large number of people. In the late nineteenth century, following some genuine medical breakthroughs, America was awash with miracle cures as opportunists sought to cash in with remedies of their own. They soon learned that a couple of people, used in the right way, could influence opinion and transform their fortunes. The show would arrive in town, providing hours of entertainment interspersed with short pitches for the nostrums. A couple of accomplices in the audience would buy the product, drink it, proclaim themselves cured, and, with animated desire, rush to buy another bottle. Soon people would be clamoring to buy whatever dubious mixture of alcohol, plant oil, herbs, and paraffin had been packaged up with an appropriately medicinal-sounding label, convinced that it would help them.[2]

Many political organizations and brand owners use market research focus groups, in the belief that they help them obtain a deeper understanding of what people think. They do so unaware that the susceptibility of people to what one or two others say and do is just as prevalent in modern-day focus groups. While it may not matter to most people if a brand of floor cleaner gets corrupted by this approach, everyone should be concerned about a research technique that shapes the national agenda of many countries when used by political parties.

The appeal of focus groups is driven by the belief that they can elicit in-depth information on a topic: by taking a group of similar people and facilitating a discussion over a protracted period of time, insights will emerge about what those people think. The theory is that, with skillful moderation, comments from one person will trigger additional thoughts from another and so on, until the group has explored its collective thoughts on the issues at hand. One advantage of groups is that a relatively large number of people (perhaps eight or more) can reach the given depth of subject exploration at the same time; another that a common view can be established giving relative efficiencies of time, ease, and cost when compared with speaking to people individually.

It is worth noting that the use of groups in psychotherapeutic work is precisely because of their capacity to affect change in people; and yet it is implicitly assumed that focus groups when used in market research don't change people at all. While the role of the therapist clearly has a part to play, the fact remains that, were he or she to be the sole point of influence in group therapy, there would be little need to put patients through the additional pain of sharing their psychological problems with strangers.

So why are we so susceptible to what other people think, how does it influence us, and why is it that, however good the moderator, focus groups generate false findings?

People can't help copying others

I have described the phenomenon of psychological priming and the problems it can cause for research. The capacity for what we've just heard to influence what we "choose" to say is part of our inadvertent capacity for copying each other. Any human interaction is a potential source of such primes, and so they are an inevitable but uncontrollable by-product of the interpersonal dynamics of a focus group. Factor in the likelihood that the subject of the discussion is often of relatively minor consequence and there is a very high probability that people will go with the conversational flow. One person choosing to talk along similar lines to the previous one isn't necessarily evidence of agreement, it's simply the nature of the way we interact.

It's not just what we hear that can cause us to follow a similar mental direction. We have a tendency to copy what others do without realizing. Evidence of this emerged in research published in the *Journal of Consumer Research*.[3] People were asked to watch a video of someone talking about a series of advertisements; in fact, the people on screen had been told to eat one of two types of cracker placed in bowls in front of them as they talked. The study found that the people watching mimicked the selection of the person talking in the video, taking the same cracker from the two choices available to them.

One aspect that can contribute dramatically to the success of any initiative is the extent to which people will copy others they see using the product or hear talking about it. This can be achieved in numerous ways: devising a tag line for an advertisement that people like to repeat, like Budweiser did with the *Wassup?* campaign; making a product's visibility integral to its appeal, as Apple did with the iPod's white headphones; creating a buzz around a product by releasing a limited amount of intriguing information about it in advance (provided you can live up to your own hype), as Hollywood likes to do when it lets it be known that a particular new movie is in production, that a particular actor has been cast, or that an on-screen romance wasn't all acting.

Fads and fashions evolve from this aspect of our desire to mirror others. For no specific reason that we can identify, a shirt that we decided we absolutely *had* to buy and used to love to wear becomes one that we choose not to put on and sometimes, eventually, one that we're embarrassed to see ourselves wearing in old pictures.

Unfortunately, focus groups don't simulate this propensity to be unknowingly influenced in a helpful way, because contextual influences and the wider canvas of day-to-day life are substituted for an entirely abstract and artificial focus on the subject of interest to the research. As a result, the copying we're so predisposed to manifests itself in the way in which people respond to the topic of the group. The impact this can have was illustrated in a brand development project I conducted recently (the "politics" of the project demanded that focus groups be used; my client shares my perspective on the inherent problems with the methodology). I was asked to gauge the potential effectiveness of a new advertising campaign using several executions that had been developed into videos comprising still images with a scripted voiceover. One of the executions featured a 1970s sitcom-style joke involving a risqué *double entendre*. When this execution was shown first, the respondents were primed to make sexual associations and went on to find sexual connotations in the other ad executions that were certainly not intended, and that were not perceived by the groups who saw these executions before the one containing the *double entendre*. I was able to anticipate and discount such blatantly primed comments, but it is not always so obvious when a prime has had an effect.

In the same advertising research, I had reached a point where the artificially rational nature of the process of deconstructing an advertising concept had, unsurprisingly, driven respondents to the point of saying that they wanted totally rational advertising: my client should simply tell them that it existed as a retailer and could provide the products it sold. Customers, the respondents were convinced, would then decide whether or not they wanted these products and act accordingly. Anxious that someone viewing the group might take what these people were saying literally, I needed to expose the artificiality of what they were seeing, so I asked the respondents to name their favorite advert. They all named ads that were nothing like the one they'd requested from my client: emotionally evocative and devoid of rational or tangible claims. More revealingly, perhaps, after the first man to speak gave a car advert as his favorite, all seven subsequent respondents mentioned car ads too; it was as though no one could think of another product category.

People change their mind to fit in with the group

Despite what we might like to tell ourselves about our pioneering and independent nature, most of our behavior comprises doing much the same as the people around us. The chances are that we'll be one of the thousands of people buying the book about an explorer that we've seen on the bestseller list, not the intrepid soul who did the actual exploring in the Amazon rainforest. The evidence shows that we can't help but care what other people think and will go to great lengths to conform.

In 1935 the pioneering social psychologist Mazafer Sherif invited people to take part in an experiment using the autokinetic effect. Participants looked at a point of light in a darkened room and were asked to report whether they thought the light was static or moving, a recreation of a natural phenomenon first observed by astronomers who thought that stars were moving. When participants were asked individually opinion was equally divided; however, when they were put into groups people tended to agree with the majority, even if this meant contradicting what they'd said originally. Later, when asked individually, they continued to subscribe to the group view. In other words, when placed in the context of a group, people will devalue their own opinion in the interest of developing an arbitrary position that is acceptable to the group.

It is relatively easy to demonstrate that an unconscious "group influence effect" exists. Get one person to stand and look at an abstract point somewhere and you will find that people take little or no notice. However, if you get three or four people doing it, virtually everybody stops to see what's so interesting.

The neuroscience of how group influence affects behavior is still in its infancy. One recent study explored the mechanisms that cause people to tend to like what their friends like. Neurologists conducted fMRI scans of teenagers' brains while they were listening to unfamiliar music spanning several genres. Each participant was played a number of songs and asked to rate how much they liked them. Then they were shown how popular the song was among a large reference group. To make sure that people weren't contrary for the sake of it, participants knew that they would receive a CD containing their favorite tracks at the end of the study.

As they expected, the researchers found that people did adjust their ratings to conform to the "popular" opinion of the tracks. However, what they discovered from brain activity through-out this process was what was so fascinating. From the areas of the brain involved (the left and right anterior insula was active in those who changed their preference), it seems that people switched their preference because they were anxious that their opinion didn't match up with those of other people. This neural activity is distinct from activity for reward and utility; in this case it seems that the music became more appealing not because it was liked or appreci-ated for its own sake, but because not liking it was worrying.[4]

One marketing case study that reflects these mental processes in action is the energy drink Red Bull. It was discovered by Austrian businessman Dietrich Mateschitz while he was traveling in Thailand. The drink, which was already called the Thai equiv-alent of Red Bull, was a cheap tonic sold by a pharmaceutical com-pany and used by factory workers to help them stay awake at work. The results of taste tests were far from positive. The market researchers concluded that no other product had ever performed so poorly in consumer testing: the look, taste, and mouth-feel were regarded as "disgusting," and the idea that it "stimulates mind and body" didn't persuade anyone that the taste was worth tolerating.[5]

When it was initially launched in Austria in 1987, the product didn't get widespread distribution. However, it became popular with clubbers and snowboarders, to whom the reviving properties appealed and who started to mix it with alcohol. Despite its being a working-man's drink in Thailand, Mateschitz set the price of Red Bull well above other soft drinks; knowing how price can alter per-ception, this almost certainly contributed to its success.

The ingredient mix of Red Bull led to a lengthy delay in its German launch while regulatory testing took place. During this time people started to talk about the product they were encountering just over the border in Austria. These discussions about whether the drink was safe were intriguing and spawned excited debate, particularly among a young adult audience that is highly disposed to risk-taking behavior. In subsequent markets the brand replicated this model of exclusivity, carefully selecting edgy venues and activities to be associated with and spurning requests from establishments and retailers that wouldn't help form the profile for the drink that the brand owner wanted to create. As recently as September 2009, two Swedish convenience store chains banned sales of Red Bull to children under 15, a move that is only likely to increase its status with young people and is unlikely to upset the company that markets it.[6]

Despite the disastrous research results Red Bull was hugely successful, having powerfully tapped into social curiosity and leveraged both priming and social proof. It wasn't just that drinking it was cool, but that there was a risk that not doing so might make you look bad to your peers. By 2006 the company had sold more than three billion cans of its "disgusting" drink, achieving sales of over €2.6 billion.

It is crucial for marketers and politicians, and anyone else who hopes to assemble a mass following, to understand the nature of group influence. However, the same influences are unrepresentatively present when a small group of people is assembled to focus on a business or political issue. No amount of careful moderation can mitigate against the fact that what you hear will be a by-product of the group dynamic rather than a reliable indication of what people in general think.

People will agree with the prevailing majority

As the nineteenth-century American salesmen discovered, the quickest way to exert intentional influence over another person is to solicit the help of a group. If several people tell someone something they will be more inclined to believe it; they may even start to doubt their own prior judgment on the matter and accept the "group" view in place of their own.

In 1953 Solomon Asch published the results of a vision test. All but one person in each group of people were "plants," who had been told by Asch to give an incorrect answer to which of three unequal lines matched another line. More than a third of the people taking part altered their answer to conform to the prevailing view; it required only that *three* other people confidently state an incorrect answer to generate this change.[7] Critics of Asch's experiment have questioned the motivation of the participants, suggesting that they modified their view because they didn't feel strongly about the issue and didn't wish to create conflict. While I accept this as a reasonable concern when considering the wider applicability of Asch's findings, I would contend that the vast majority of market research involves topics about which it would be unreasonable to expect the participants to be strongly motivated (indeed, one might worry if they were).

More recently, Dr. Gregory Burns took Asch's work a stage further using brain scans. As before, a group was constructed with a number of people in on the experiment who had been primed to provide uniformly correct or incorrect answers, and an unwitting participant who was genuinely attempting to match the rotated geometric shapes that Burns was using in the "test." What the brain imaging showed was that when people gave answers after being influenced by the group they weren't making a conscious decision to go along with what they had heard, they had actually come to believe that what the group had claimed was true.

Where organizations can convince someone that lots of people think something is worth doing or having, they tend to do well. Being the "most popular" brand, being used by an impressively large number of people, or publishing lots of positive reviews or testimonials all provide social proof that we should think something is good.

Focus groups frequently produce a unified view on a subject when observation of the diverse nature of personal taste would make it apparent that such cohesion is extremely unlikely. The commonality is a result of the format of the research, rather than a true meeting of minds. Sony Ericsson discovered this to its cost when, alongside one of the main networks (carriers), it used focus groups to assess the appeal of a new handset, the W600, among American consumers. The results would determine whether the carrier took the handset and would be used to help forecast likely demand. Consumers weren't particularly impressed and the carrier very nearly didn't take the phone at all. In the end, the carrier decided that it would take it and forecast sales of just 5,000 units for the first quarter. When the handset hit the market, 10,000 were sold in the first fortnight and ten times the original estimate were sold in the first quarter. As one Sony Ericsson worker described it:

> The amount of back orders and supply chain havoc this caused was a nightmare. Our final forecast would indicate around 75,000 pcs would have been sold if we'd been able to meet demand.

It only needed one or two people to express a negative view of the new phone and others followed. Whether they were primed by someone drawing their attention to one less than compelling feature, a strong familiarity and preference for a competing product, or a bad experience with one of Sony Ericsson's products in the past, it just so happened that a negative consensus prevailed.

When it comes to considering a new product's potential success in a market, it's worth reflecting on the basic math of the matter. How many people in a group did Sony Ericsson *need* to like its new phone? Apple's iPhone is rightly regarded as a huge success and yet, one year after it was launched, its share of the smartphone market was around 10%.[8] Sony Ericsson's phone was never aiming for such a dominant share of the market, but even if it was, it only required that one person in each group be sufficiently enthusiastic about it to decide to buy one in the subsequent 12 months.

Some market researchers might point out that it is wrong to allow a qualitative methodology to gauge the potential market for a product. However, such techniques are routinely used to screen initial ideas prior to wider development, at which point a product that one person present likes will be swiftly abandoned. In any event, the same basic mathematics applies with a quantitative approach: few companies are going to launch a product that only 5% of respondents say they will buy, and yet this may be all that is required (or all that can be achieved) in the first quarter of a new product's life.

Discussions change attitudes

As long ago as 1961, James Stoner found that people changed their attitudes after discussing a subject with a small group of people.[9] David Myers and Helmut Lamm conducted an extensive review of research into group discussions and found substantial evidence that they have a polarizing effect on the people who take part in them across a wide variety of situations. When people lean in one way or another when considering something individually, discussion with a group tends to amplify that opinion: by the end of the discussion a relatively minor preference or dislike will become a much stronger one. The reason for this is interesting. Research suggests that people enter a group discussion with a misconception of the position of the other participants; they tend to assume that they will have a stronger view than the group, and to have an ideal position that is more extreme than the one they're prepared to voice. When the arguments raised in the group discussion support the initial position, people feel a need to shift their declared position in that direction.

In other words, we like to perceive ourselves as more in the socially preferred direction than the people we compare ourselves with. It seems that we run a constant mental scorecard assessing what the social average is, to make sure that we position ourselves just above it.

Interestingly, reading or listening to arguments generally produces less effect than actual participation in the discussion. It has been suggested that it's the mental process of actively rehearsing or reformulating an argument that brings about the shift in position; through the process of expressing it to others, we convince ourselves of our own argument.[10] Building influence by instigating debate around a subject or brand is what makes viral marketing and political blogging so effective. When the topic is skillfully released or the fuse of debate lit in the right way, the resulting impact can be dramatic.

The challenge for focus groups is compounded by the frequently humdrum subject matter on which they focus. It is one thing to feel that you will stand your ground in a debate with strangers about the death penalty or a solution to the problems in the Middle East, but the packaging of a breakfast cereal or your reaction to a new biscuit is not something most people are likely to feel passionate about. Research analyzing discussion content has shown that the largest shifts in attitudes occur where the subject matter is mundane and the argument put forward novel. Many focus groups will *create* the attitudes they report, rather than reflect views that are representative of people who haven't taken part in the discussions facilitated for the research process.[11]

A persuasive voice in the crowd

Often a moderator is seeking a sense of agreement from the group about a topic: how a brand is perceived or positioned, the merits of a new product, the appeal of an advertising campaign. If several people offer a similar opinion on a topic, it seems reasonable to surmise that that opinion is widely held and to report it as such. However, social psychologists have experimented and found that just one person repeating a point of view several times is very nearly as influential as several people making the same point independently.[12] There is a real risk that someone listening to a group will be swayed not by an actual consensus, but by one repetitive voice. This should come as no surprise to companies that advertise: part of what makes a message effective is the number of times people get to hear it.

The way in which a point is made by another group member will also contribute dramatically to the extent to which it influences the others present. It's not only the tone of voice that makes a point more commanding and influential, the nature of the point itself has been shown to change the extent to which people are influenced by it. When a statement is presented as something that could or should have been evident beforehand, people revise their attitudes and intentions as though they really did know whatever it was in advance.[13]

Just how persuasive one voice can be was illustrated in a fascinating article by Robert Harley, editor of *The Absolute Sound*, a high-end audiophile equipment and music review magazine. He described a blind audio test conducted by Swedish Radio, which wanted to establish if one of a number of low-bit-rate codecs (systems to compress and play back music) was good enough to replace FM broadcasting in Europe. A careful "double-blind, triple stimulus, hidden reference" test was constructed, in which 60 "expert" listeners would make more than 20,000 evaluations each, involving first listening to the unprocessed signal and then hearing two other versions of the same music; they were asked to identify which had been processed by the codec. Eventually, Swedish Radio had narrowed down its search to only two codecs, both of which were believed to be good enough to replace analog FM broadcasts. The test seemed extremely thorough, totally unbiased, and entirely fair.

However, after reaching its conclusions Swedish Radio sent a tape that had been compressed using the new codec to an acknowledged expert in digital audio, Bart Locanthi, who listened to the track knowing that it had been subject to compression. He immediately identified that the compression had introduced a distortion. When he told Swedish Radio what he had found its staff had no trouble hearing the same issue for themselves. In a few minutes he'd identified what all those blind tests had failed to appreciate.[14] Irrespective of what all the people concerned had thought when listening in one set of circumstances, one voice had caused them to reevaluate their opinion.

What can work so effectively as a marketing technique undermines focus groups as an objective tool for exploring what people think. Knowing how influenced people can be by one person, particularly someone perceived as expert or a celebrity with whom they feel an affinity, provides a powerful mechanism for shaping perceptions of your brand. For example, in the early 1990s Pizza Hut wanted to give its brand a lift. It successfully used a number of different celebrities in its advertisements, from super-models to racing drivers. As a result, people who had previously not considered visiting the restaurants changed their opinion and sales started to climb.

Conversely, in a focus group, one well argued, novel, or authoritatively expressed point can sway the entire outcome of the debate, even though those taking part feel certain that their views are their own and not a consequence of what they've heard in the group itself. Rarely do all the people present have the same degree of experience and commitment to a topic. The focus group format – whereby a question or topic is put to the group and the group is invited to respond – encourages the person with the strongest involvement and view and/or the most confident person present to speak first. The process fosters the emergence of a leader and one person's opinion frequently influences the responses of others.

Groupthink: The perils of thinking together

When a group of people make decisions jointly or work together to reach a conclusion about something, there is a risk of group-think, a phenomenon first explained in detail by American psychologist Irving Janis back in the 1970s. He realized that groups making decisions had the capacity to reach those decisions with insufficient critical analysis and with too much deference to the prevailing point of view. This, he explained, had contributed to a number of political fiascoes, such as the failure to prepare adequately for the Pearl Harbour attack, the Cuban Missile Crisis, and the attempted cover-up of the Watergate scandal. Both Lord Butler's 2004 Review of Intelligence of Mass Destruction in the UK and Senator Pat Roberts' intelligence review in the US cited group-think as a factor in the failure of the intelligence behind the decision to invade Iraq.

When one considers the elements that contribute to these infamous decisions, it's easy to draw parallels with consumer focus groups. Janis identified eight symptoms of groupthink:

1 *The illusion of invulnerability creates excessive optimism that encourages risk taking.* It's hard to conceive of a more invulnerable group than a consumer focus group. If they like the product, ad, or whatever is being tested, they're under no compunction even to part with the few pounds the product would cost; in fact, under the UK Market Research Society's code of conduct, it's understandably important that the line between selling and research is kept very clear.

2 *Collective rationalization – discounting warnings that might challenge the group's assumptions, rather than reconsidering them.* The goal of most group facilitators is to arrive at a consensus view (even if only unconsciously because it will make writing the report easier). Combine this with problems caused by priming and people's tendency to want to stick with what they've said rather than risk being perceived as inconsistent (cognitive consistency theory), and the propensity for collective rationalization is certainly present.

3 *Unquestioning belief in the morality of the group causes members to ignore the consequences of their actions.* In my experience few respondents are self-critically judgmental in focus groups, being far too preoccupied with how they're being perceived by the strangers that comprise the rest of the group. However, the problems are compounded by the fact that there are no consequences (to the respondents) of their focus group comments. While making respondents legally responsible for subsequent marketing failures is an interesting notion, it's possible that research response rates would drop!

4 *Stereotyping those outside who are opposed to the group in a derogatory way.* Resistance to ideas from the company behind whatever is being investigated may hinder concepts that may be persuasive under other circumstances.

5 *Direct pressure on dissenters – members are put under pressure not to express arguments that go against the group's views.* Again, not many people are willing to make a stand on principle for a consumer issue that they consider either insignificant or academic in the face of several people opining a contrary argument.

6 *Self-censorship of ideas that deviate from the group consensus.* I've already discussed the polarizing nature of groups. The desire for social cohesion works in a number of directions, and one would have to question how strongly a respondent would need to feel about a topic in a consumer focus group to introduce disharmony.

7 *The illusion of unanimity among group members – people take silence as agreement.* Rarely, if ever, does a research moderator actively canvas the opinions of everyone present, not least because it would break the flow of discussion and create a very unnatural interaction that would work against the primary goal of the focus group (i.e., to get people talking about the issue in question).

8 *Self-appointed mind guards who shield the group from dissenting information.*

Leaving aside point 8, which I would say only applies with the worst of focus group moderators, and point 2, which I concede is marginal, there is an argument to say that six of Janis's eight symptoms of groupthink are present in focus groups. The propensity for a focus group to reach a "bad" conclusion is therefore significant.

It should go without saying after the issues raised in Chapter 3 that the context, whereby a number of consumers are placed together in a room to talk about something, bears little relationship to the environment in which a consumer's response would normally occur. The artificial focus of discussing a consumer issue for a long period is a recipe for distortion and it's all too easy for that focus to miss the point entirely, either because the consumer response isn't determined at this level of mental processing, or simply because the abstract nature of the discussion means that something that seems irrelevant is glossed over. However, if all of this weren't enough, the market research world has conspired to create a way of making focus groups even more artificial: the viewing facility.

Convenience wins over truth (again)

If the arguments and supporting science provided up to this point have convinced you (as I hope they have) that the environment influences how people think and behave, then what follows will come as no surprise. Nevertheless, the widespread use of viewing facilities and the flagrant way in which they ignore human psychology mean that they merit inclusion in this book.

I accept that some of the emerging evidence on the extent to which the unconscious drives our behavior, and our inability to post-rationalize it accurately, isn't intuitively apparent. Indeed, it can be quite uncomfortable discovering how extensive is the illusion of conscious will (to use Daniel Wegner's phrase). However, I don't believe that most of the inherent issues with viewing facilities should be so unapparent, and in many ways they serve to illustrate the extremes of artificiality that are widely accepted in market research. It's as if someone sat down and thought: "OK, how can I find a way of finding out what people think that is as unrealistic as possible?"

For the uninitiated, viewing facilities are specially constructed to provide a room in which research can be conducted, usually with 10 or 12 comfortable chairs, a coffee table, and a television (for showing stimulus material such as advertisements). Almost one whole wall of the room is replaced by a two-way mirror (sometimes confusingly called a one-way mirror), on the other side of which is a second room in which a similar number of observers can watch the proceedings without being visible to the respondents. Sound is captured by microphones in the respondent room, and in almost all cases there are one or two video cameras to record the conversation.

So far so good, you may think. However, in order for the observers to remain invisible to the respondents, it is necessary to keep the respondent room very brightly lit, while the observers sit in semi-darkness. In addition, and just in case it wasn't obvious from the cameras and microphones, respondents are told (normally verbally and through signs in the room) that they are being videoed and recorded. Which of us, hand on heart, honestly believes that we would be ourselves in such an environment? There are more than 150 such facilities in the UK and over 600 in the US, charging several hundred dollars per group. Some larger manufacturing organizations use them so frequently that they have invested in their own viewing facilities.

As is so often the case with market research, the convenience of hearing consumers say something is accepted irrespective of the probable reliability of what's heard. Let's explore why the results are likely to be unreliable.

Get ready to think

Viewing facilities manage to create problems even before the first topic is raised for discussion. Long before respondents reach the artificial reality of the comfortable chair in the bright, mirrored room, they have to deal with arriving at the "facility." If you spend any time observing people moving from one space to another, you will see that they change pace as they make a transition from one area to the next. They make unconscious adjustments from whatever was in their mind as they traveled – getting to the right destination, being on time, anticipating what will happen there – to sizing up their new surroundings. This is an element that good designers are adept at influencing to suit their goals; in retail environments it can help encourage customers to engage with more products more quickly and spend longer in the store. Most viewing facilities inadvertently create the feeling of entering a secret government compound! Because they are secured behind door-entry systems – it would be impractical to have a staffed entrance – respondents arrive and announce themselves over an intercom to an unseen receptionist. There then follows a series of stairs and/or corridors to reach the first holding area, or in the case of one manufacturer-owned facility, a seven-floor journey in an elevator.

To the best of my knowledge, no one has studied how such an entry influences what people say, but given the ways in which subtle environmental factors shape the way people respond, it is hard to conceive that they wouldn't. Even if such an arrival is soon forgotten, the use of a mirror, having people watching, recording equipment, and light levels all demonstrably do change how people think.

Magic mirror on the wall

The mirror, essential to the viewing experience, is a problem because it, too, changes how people think and behave. Most people are surprised (for me it's unpleasantly) when they see themselves on video, because when we consciously look in a mirror we don't usually see ourselves as we are. If we are psychologically healthy we will filter out the negatives and fix on the parts of ourselves we like; if not, we will either fixate on the parts we don't like, or else like ourselves so much we become unbearable to others. This mechanism enables people to buy clothes that don't suit them, and that they would view disparagingly on others, simply because they only look at one aspect when they try them on. The same mechanism, albeit to an extreme degree, enables an anorexic to see themselves and still think they need to be thinner.

On such a scale, and when seated in front of it, a viewing facility mirror works more like the unwelcome and unflattering video of oneself, providing occasional reflections to sensitize respondents to their unconscious expressions and mannerisms.

"Does this self-awareness necessarily change anything?" I hear you ask. The evidence suggests that it does. Having spent hours and hours observing consumers in retail places, Paco Underhill realized that when people pass shiny surfaces they slow down, but when there are too many reflective surfaces it becomes disorientating.[15] When Arthur Beaman and his colleagues set up an experiment on Halloween to see if the presence of a mirror altered the amount of candy children took while believing that they were unobserved, they found that children who had a reflection of themselves at the time were far less likely to take more than they'd been instructed to.[16] Another study found that the performance of people copying foreign text was improved by the presence of a mirror.[17] Diener and Walborn reduced the proportion of students who cheated on a test by taking extra time at the end from 70% to just 7%; the only difference was the presence of a mirror.[18]

Somebody's watching you

Given that people behave differently when they're observing themselves, it's no surprise that they do so when they know they're being watched by others. Aside from the expected increase in self-awareness and self-consciousness, I have also found that it can increase defensiveness and aggression, particularly in men. Research by anesthesiologists found that patients who were told they were being observed changed their behavior during and after surgery, including the amount of pain they felt after surgery (people being observed felt less). The study concluded that the action of observing patients in clinical trials could invalidate the results of an experiment.[19]

Staring at the light

The bright lighting in the respondent room that is necessary to allow the two-way mirror to function properly exerts its own influence on respondents. Countless research papers have studied the impact that the level and type of light have on people, including the Hawthorne research discussed overleaf.[20]

Essentially, our bodies are regulated by light levels and we have a circadian rhythm repeating approximately every 24 hours for cycles of sleep/wakefulness, body temperature, hormone production, and alertness. With such a fundamental link between our physiology and light, it isn't surprising that studies have found differences in behavior and mood when light levels are varied. At the most simplistic level, more light is associated with greater engagement and, in work environments, higher output levels. For example, one study found that sensitivity to an unpleasant noise increased as the level of illumination was increased.[21]

A recipe for inaccuracy

The sum impact of the viewing facility environment is to induce a sense of hyper-consciousness, dramatically at odds with how most consumer behavior occurs. The transition through an entrance system that often involves consciously expressing the reason the respondent is there; the journey along unfamiliar corridors to a room in which respondents are told that they are being watched, filmed, and audio recorded; being observed by unseen strangers in a room that is brightly lit and where a large mirror reflects how others will be seeing them – there are not, from my perspective, a recipe for discovering consumer truths. Short of having a silent observer standing right next to each respondent, I struggle to conceive of a way of creating a research environment more at odds with consumer reality.

Typically, when people refer to the Hawthorne effect it is to support the view that a variation occurs in how people behave when they know they are being observed; in the experiments, researchers looked at how the productivity of workers changed under different environmental conditions (initially changes in levels of lighting). Since the original projects were conducted, several other studies have examined the research and suggested that the changes in productivity could be attributable to other variables. However, it is interesting to consider all the variables that *could* have accounted for the changes in production observed at the Hawthorne factory:[22]

◆ Different light levels affected productivity.
◆ Impromptu team work among the participants increased their effectiveness.
◆ Being studied influenced the participants' degree of motivation.
◆ Feedback from the measurement of their work enhanced the skills of the participants.

In a viewing facility the first three of these influences will almost certainly be present, and there is a reasonable argument to say that the presence (and impact) of the moderator is analogous to the fourth.

The wrong way and the right way to think about groups

When Sony Ericsson realized how much money it had lost as a result of the focus groups it ran on the W600 handset, it was forced to reconsider the use of such groups. Evidently up until that point the tacit belief had been that asking groups of consumers what they thought was a reliable gauge of something. While a few companies have moved away from them, virtually every research agency that describes itself as expert in qualitative methods offers focus groups as a legitimate market research tool. Consequently, numerous products, services, and pieces of marketing communication make it to market or are rejected because of feedback from groups of consumers interviewed collectively. There remains a notion that prompting a discussion with other consumers present will reveal more thoughts and feelings than might otherwise be identified, and of course such groups are quick and convenient to conduct.

Our own illusions of conscious control no doubt contribute to the perspective that we know we could be asked to discuss *our* opinion on something with a group of strangers and would ruthlessly stick to our beliefs; after all, we know what *we* think.

Much of the criticism of focus groups – and there has been a lot – involves issues with respondent recruitment. Are the people who are willing to participate necessarily representative of the market as a whole? Are they "professional respondents" who take part in such discussions with great frequency for the payment provided to participants? Others have pointed out that for a supposedly in-depth research tool the amount of discussion time per participant can be insubstantial: 12 respondents taking part in a standard 90-minute group discussion would have an average of 7.5 minutes of airtime each, less when any introductions or warm-up discussions are included.

However, these are moot points if any group inherently distorts what respondents think and say. When people think differently in groups, need to feel more strongly about a subject to stand up for it in a group situation, unconsciously allow their attitudes and what they focus on to be altered, become more vehement and are primed by what they hear other people say, it doesn't matter how well the respondents are recruited or how expertly the group is moderated.

There are many reasons to believe that the information emanating from focus groups is a by-product of the group dynamics through which it has been collected, far more than that it is an accurate reflection of the consumer response of those same people in the real world. Given the relatively mundane nature of consumer research topics, any reasonable comment or reaction raised by a respondent in a group discussion is likely to face little opposition from the other people present. In psychological terms, the very fact that it has been voiced first will give it additional impact.

All of these problems are compounded by the issues I've discussed in previous chapters regarding the perils of artificial introspection and the potential impact of a moderator's behavioral style unconsciously encouraging a particular type of response. The need to encourage respondents to feel comfortable and to open up is a recipe for the "please you" behavior driver, which encourages an upbeat response.

If accurate consumer insights are the objective, then by far the simplest "solution" is to avoid focus groups altogether. The only theoretical place for them would be if researchers believed that they could simulate the complex social influence that occurs in human groups. In such circumstances, hearing the group interaction take place *may* be illuminating. However, this isn't a justification for recruiting a group of people who don't know one another and moderating a discussion between them. Instead, the aim should be to take an existing social group, put them in the most accurate context possible, subtly release the initiative in their presence (and in the presence of as much of its competition as possible), and stand back and see what happens. Even then, the problems of the tacit leader's views dominating the discussion or inadvertent priming taking it in a particular direction mean that it can't be relied on.

When the Post Office decided to rebrand itself to create an identity that would reflect all of the things it did as a business and would work internationally, it reportedly spent more than £2 million on the process. It stated that the new name, Consignia, was "extremely well received in customer research." Nevertheless, it was lambasted by the press; it seemed to be a word, but no one was sure what it meant. Worse still, UK consumers had a long and broadly affectionate relationship with the Post Office and felt like they were losing something fundamental. As you know by now, loss aversion is a powerful motivating force. Understanding the true nature of consumer behavior would have been far more valuable than whatever was wasted on market research.[23]

By all means, if the subject of interest is what people talk about when placed in a brightly lit room while being watched by a hidden group of strangers, use a viewing facility. Otherwise, using one is unlikely to be beneficial.

For the most part, the best way to consider groups is in terms of the role that social influence has on consumer behavior. As I've discussed in previous chapters, people are hugely susceptible to priming and to social proof. The appeal of a product or new brand name can be hugely influenced by who says it's good or who is seen to be using it, irrespective of its apparent merits when considered consciously.

The truth is that consumer behavior, just like all human behavior, is very much a by-product of the wider social group. Understanding how the right combination of context and group influence can lead to commercial success (or the absence of it) is perhaps as close to defining a magic formula for marketing new products as it is possible to get. However, such studying of group interactions has to take place unobtrusively in the native habitat of the consumer, or else be considered in the broader context of the way we behave in relation to one another. It can't be recreated artificially in a couple of hours with a moderator in a strange room.

Going back to the example of New Coke that I discussed previously, the group influence effect was another significant factor in Coca-Cola's undoing. Inevitably, Coke's customers didn't carry out an independent, balanced assessment of the new recipe's qualities as the research respondents had done: they heard the media, friends, and colleagues talking about it. The sentiment started to spread that the removal of the old recipe was somehow undermining the essence of America; one newspaper columnist compared changing the drink's formulation to the removal of President Roosevelt's face from Mount Rushmore.[24] Demonstrating admirable, if misguided, faith, Coke's executives continued to take comfort from the surveys they were conducting that told them people liked the new flavor. Instead, people were leaning toward loss aversion and copying the sentiment of those around them who were saying that something significant was being taken away. Ultimately, the group decided that it didn't like the *idea* of what Coca-Cola was doing, and that mattered far more than what they as individuals might have thought of the actual taste.

Understanding the reasons that focus groups can't help shed light on what people really think or do in itself provides a checklist against which to consider an initiative that you might, misguidedly, have asked such a group to evaluate:

Focus groups don't work because...	About your initiative...
People copy each other.	Will it be visible?
People change their mind to fit in.	Will people feel they must have it?
People agree with the majority.	Can you win over enough people early on?
Discussion changes attitudes.	Can you get people talking about it?
One voice can sway the group.	Can you get experts or ambassadors on side?

One of the most popular applications for focus groups is exploring what people want and whether they like a product, policy, or piece of communication. This raises the question: Is there a reliable way of asking people what they would like in the future?

8

CONSUMER FUTUROLOGY

Influencing innovation

It's a mistake to ask people what they think they want. As Henry Ford said, "If I had asked my customers what they wanted, they would have said a faster horse." Although some may even have balked at that, saying they were very happy with the horse they already had (particularly if they had only just bought it). Similarly, it's a mistake to ask people what they think about a new product, service, or marketing idea and let their collective opinion shape yours. When market research wanders into the realm of the future it is inherently reckless.

Most of the examples I have referenced in this book have involved an element of research futurology: the attempt to create a New Coke that consumers will love more than another product; the number of people who will decide they want to visit the Millennium Dome; whether enough people will decide they like Red Bull, Baileys, a Sony Ericsson mobile phone, or an advert for beer. While they highlight failings with the research process whatever its focus, they serve as useful examples because real life has had the opportunity to prove them wrong. The scientific understanding that has emerged in recent years from social psychology and neuroscience shows that most research is an exercise in wishful thinking. The only thing market research guarantees is that you will get some answers, not that they will be an accurate reflection of people's motivations, needs, or desires.

Fortunately there is sufficient research agnosticism for people occasionally to trust their instincts, discount what research says, and go ahead anyway and, as a result, evidence of such research failings occasionally finds its way into the public domain. However, the vast scale of the research industry is testimony to the fact that hope of obtaining reassurance that a decision is good before it's taken overpowers the experiences that show it can't.

This is hardly a unique example of wishful thinking in the human condition: religion propagates the implausible but desirable notion of life after death, astrology that the positioning of celestial bodies can explain the present and predict the future, and homeopathy that the more diluted a substance is, the more potent its remedial properties will be. History shows that people are quite willing to embrace an idea if it is comforting and discount or discard experiences that undermine it.

There are companies who acknowledge that it is incumbent on them to make decisions about what to create, embracing their legitimate position as the ultimate arbiters of expertise and custodians of their own brand. The car manufacturer Porsche has never sought customer opinions of its car designs; it recognizes that it is for the company to determine if something is right. The benefit of its approach is evidenced by the Porsche Cayenne SUV. The car received very mixed reviews, with many experts deciding that it was ugly. However, through Porsche staying true to the visual cues that appealed to the 911 buyers who were buying competitors' SUVs as family cars and giving people time to get used to seeing the design, the car became successful, and within a year was outselling every other model the company made.[1]

BMW's radical redesign of its 5 series in 2003 led to mixed reviews from industry pundits. However, within half a decade many competitors' new cars were echoing elements of the BMW design, and those that didn't were starting to look distinctly oldfashioned. The German car manufacturer works hard to understand its customers, but it knows that it can't rely on them to shape design. As BMW's design director explained in an interview with the Wall Street Journal in 2008, the company would be asking customers to make judgments based on the world today, whereas the designs need to appeal to them eight years later.[2]

Perhaps the most ironic example of research futurology I've encountered occurred when the BBC explored the idea of commissioning a new version of the classic science fiction series Doctor Who, a programme about a "time lord" who makes frequent trips into the future. According to the show's writer, "the research found that no one wanted to watch *Doctor Who*. Kids said it was a programme for their parents. The parents said it was a dead show. I expected it to die a death after a year." The research had concluded that the program was a niche show for sci-fi geeks.[3] Program controllers ignored the findings and produced the program anyway, and over the last five years it has been a huge BBC ratings success. The BBC might just as well have asked the fictitious doctor whether people would watch him in the future.

Research alchemy

In most walks of life people are understandably skeptical about claims of an ability to predict the future accurately. While some fall for the vague generalities proffered by astrologers and psychics, such practices have never fared well when subjected to scientific scrutiny. They are perpetuated because of the victims' (or as the practitioners of these dark arts might describe them, clients') unhealthy levels of confirmation bias regarding whatever mystical package the forecast has been wrapped in: they will attribute importance only to the times the predictions are right and dismiss those that aren't as irrelevancies.

Market research routinely makes the implicit claim that it works as a tool to see into the future. Will customers buy a particular product? Will they buy it again? Which packaging will encourage them to purchase more or more often? Will they come back to a shop, restaurant, or venue again? How will they vote in an election? All these depend on the notion that the response to some abstract stimulus, be it a question or a real-life example taken entirely out of context, can be relied on as an indicator of what will happen at some later point in time; all are contingent on the capacity of each respondent to predict the future.

The basis for this "faith" in consumer research must stem from one of two alternative hypotheses: either that if you ask people what they like now, they will tell you honestly and it will remain constant in the future; or that if you ask people what they will do in the future, they will tell you honestly and then go on to do what they've said they'll do.

The desire to predict the future is an understandable one, and one into which much time, effort, and money is invested. In the late 1980s I was working for one of the UK's largest financial services organizations in its research and planning department. An econometric model of the UK housing market had been commissioned at considerable expense from one of the world's leading management consultancies. After statistically modeling all of the available data a statistically accurate model of the market was obtained, illustrated by a chart with two very closely matched lines; one showing the actual average house price and the other the one predicted by the model. While the technical basis for such a model is to explain the movement in the data historically, the appeal is its ability to forecast what will happen in the future, and this was very much the focus of attention when the model arrived. Unfortunately, within a few weeks the stock market crashed and house prices started to fall dramatically; within four years the average price of a property had halved (a 35% drop in real terms). The model hadn't foretold the crash and couldn't explain it.

So is the faith in consumer research's ability to predict the future justified? Can consumers reliably tell us what they will do in the future?

We don't know what we will think in the future

In Chapter 1 I explained how our behavior is frequently unconsciously driven, and that we have no direct access to the mental processes that influence what we do so dramatically. It's no surprise that if we have no access to such processes when the events are "live," we can't be expected to forecast how we will behave under their influence in the future.

When people are asked to imagine how they would feel if something fantastic or terrible happened to them, they invariably exaggerate the extent of their response. Many people would love to win the lottery and believe that they would take the sudden transformation to having great wealth in their stride. And yet there are a surprising number of well-documented cases of big winners who held such views when they bought their ticket finding life no happier and sometimes much more difficult once they've received the multimillion-pound check. I know someone who inherited a successful manufacturing business and a vast amount of money. While he had the wealth to take whatever holidays he pleased, could drive the car of his dreams, and buy an amazing house, he suffered huge stress in managing the business – something he was poorly equipped to do. Further anxiety ensued about how his wealth should best be invested and, when his investments performed poorly, the magnified distress of knowing he'd lost a significant sum of money as a result. He hadn't anticipated any of these issues and it seemed that all the advantages his new-found wealth provided were counter-balanced by something he found difficult to deal with.

Social psychologists have conducted research that supports this perspective on our ability to anticipate our futures accurately. It seems that we have a tempering psychological mechanism for positive and negative events. While people seek out happiness, as soon as it is attained its value declines; when sadness occurs it tends not to stay for as long as people predict.[4] In time, people return to their personal baseline level of contentment come what may. The same tempering mechanism that helps us overcome grief also removes the shine from happy events. When the unexpected happens people work to make sense of the events, and in doing so the impact that was novel becomes more familiar and more standard as a result. In this way the shock of attending a first car-crash fatality helps ameliorate the experience for paramedics, rather than letting the effect of subsequent experiences be compounded emotionally.

Such processes aren't predictable or consciously applied. Most of us would, I'm sure, prefer to retain the euphoric feeling of a winning lottery ticket or the triumphal victory of our favorite sporting team for far longer. In one sense I should have been far more disappointed than I was that the Euro 2008 soccer tournament was taking place without the England team. However, rather than each match serving as a reminder of what I was missing, I was able to enjoy the absence of stress that each match would have involved had my own nation been represented. Before the start of the tournament I *thought* I would have no interest in it; the press campaigns asking me who I would support were a reminder that the team I supported wouldn't be playing! However, when the Dutch team hammered the Italians in their first group match I found the combination of attractive soccer, connections to friends in the country, and our positive historic national relationship with the Netherlands a sound basis from which to cheer them on. I would never have anticipated it would happen, but I soon found myself making the same diary space to watch the games in which the Dutch were playing as I would have done had England been participating.

Again, studies suggest my experience is normal. People taking part in an experiment where they received unflattering feedback from a personality test predicted their negative reactions would last much longer than they actually did, a phenomenon known as durability bias.[5] Research by Timothy Wilson also found that American college football fans thought that the result of a game would influence their happiness for two or three days, but by the following day they were back to their usual level of contentment.[6]

One could argue that people will be able to state the direction of their feeling accurately: they know they will feel good or bad, they just overestimate to what extent. The problem when using consumer research to gauge feelings about, say, using a new product when it is launched is that the strength of feeling will determine how people behave. The feeling for the product needs to be strong enough to bring about the change in behavior required to purchase it. But people aren't conscious of this requirement and, as a result, the mechanisms they use to forecast how they will feel in the future aren't accurate.

Using a telescope to see what lies ahead: Focalism

Imagine you are given a gun to shoot a golf ball that you know is approximately 200 yards away from you, but you don't know where. You have a powerful rifle with an equally powerful telescopic sight, so once you've found the ball, shooting it will be straightforward. The problem with using a telescopic sight is that it is very good at giving a close-up image of the thing you are looking at, but very bad (hopeless in fact) at putting that image into its context. You may be able to see a small white ball magnified to a useful-sized target when you've found it, but locating the target either requires looking at everything in view with the naked eye (virtually impossible) or sweeping the magnified image back and forth looking at each square foot of ground one "picture" at a time. This must be the reason that, even in America, frustrated golfers don't carry the ballistic means to vent their frustration at wayward shots.

Using market research to explore the future suffers from a similar problem, known as focalism. When considering the future people routinely fail to take into account everything that is going on in their life at any given time and focus too much on the issue being considered. They think too much about how something could happen, and too little about how and why it might not.[7] It's not just the "focus" of a focus group that creates this type of bias, almost every form of consumer research seeks to take customers through a process that has them analyze elements of purchase decisions, concentrating on different aspects of the consumer issue in question. In part, this is a by-product of a process that seeks to rationalize what is often largely or partially not rational, but it is also the result of the way in which the research process is structured. Getting respondents can be time-consuming and so it seems prudent to squeeze them for information, be it through the depth of interviewing, the duration of the discussion, or the number of questions they are asked. The decisions that companies have to make are usually complex and involve numerous elements spanning the responsibilities of several departments and external agencies: manufacturing want to know if their product is liked, marketing that their proposition for it will be well received, finance that the price will be sufficient, and so on. Each of these issues has a multitude of subsidiary questions: How is each element of the product received? How well does it function? Could it be made better? Each respondent will be required to consider every aspect that the company commissioning the research has to consider, however fleeting and superficial their real involvement with that product would be in reality. The more people focus on something (or are required to focus on something because of the research process they're participating in), the more likely they are to ignore factors that will have a bearing on the issue when it actually happens.

The power of novelty

Last week I took my children to a local zoo. In the café we stopped at for lunch, the children's food arrived in an animal-themed cardboard box and included a cheap animal toy. After a small amount of inter-child toy envy and negotiation with the kind woman at the checkout, both ended up with a six-inch rubber snake. Despite having a monetary value of just a few pence, in the eyes of a 6- and a 3-year-old child these were the most desirable items on the planet. Twenty minutes later, when it transpired that one snake was missing in a play area the size of a football field, I knew that no amount of discussion about the financial worth, meagre quality, or inauthentic design of the item was going to cut it with my daughter, and I was either going to have to start a search of forensic proportions, or else buy another lunch that no one wanted in the hope that there was still a snake available that could be traded for whatever toy came in the box. The experience was all the more frustrating (until I found the snake by chance) because I knew that the novelty would soon wear off. Seven days later I can report that I haven't seen the snakes; my children have no idea where they are and have no interest in looking for them.

As is so often the case, what one observes in children is an amplified version of a trait we all have to a greater or lesser degree. When we see something for the first time it has an appeal borne of its newness that will, over time, dissipate. We wouldn't be the extraordinarily creative, progressive, and successful species that we are if we weren't intrinsically attracted to new things.

One factor that can temper our propensity for novelty bias is our aversion to risk. However, when being asked to evaluate something for the purposes of research there is no risk. There is no purchase to be made, no money to be spent, and no previously favored alternative to reject as a result of selecting the new alternative.

Breaking with convention

People are creatures of habit. Perhaps because of the natural cycles of life on an orbiting planet, our lives are divided into neat sections of hours within days within seasons within years, compounded by the semi-fixed physiological requirements for food and sleep. Our days become routine filled, and most people can, for any point in the near future, predict with reasonable accuracy where they will be and what, broadly, they will be doing.

When we make new decisions – real decisions with consequences, not those requested by consumer research – we experience anxiety. Will the decision prove to be a good one? Our unconscious mind plays its role in making us aware of the potential risks of whatever we're considering. Once that new decision is made, and repeated, and no bad event befalls us because of it, we develop a sense of faith about our choice. For example, when I lived in North London I had to park my car on the road overnight. When the obvious (convenient) choice of the road I lived on had no spaces I had a choice about which road I selected as an alternative. The first time I chose an unfamiliar road I was anxious about the risks. Would the car be OK? Would the slightly rougher-looking buildings house people whose idea of a good night out was to vandalize my car? When I found the car undamaged the following morning I felt better about my choice, and with each vandalism-free night my car enjoyed, so my faith in the place I'd chosen to park increased. Very quickly I didn't have to think about where to park my car if my own road was full; the second road was fine. As it turned out it was on a day when I had been able to park on my own road that, as I walked back home from the train station, I watched someone stroll up to my car and smash the wing mirror off.

What we really choose (as opposed to what we think we'll choose when we've been asked) has much to do with what's easiest, and that, very often is just a case of doing what we've done before. This is one the ways in which advertising changes what we buy: through repeatedly seeing a product in an advert it becomes unconsciously familiar and we are correspondingly more favorable to it. And only the unconscious needs to notice the ad; research shows that conscious awareness of having been exposed to something isn't a prerequisite for this fluency bias to occur.[8] I suspect that the unconscious mind is duped into concluding that something it has encountered on several occasions without coming to harm is "safe." This mechanism of unconsciously accepting familiar things would have made sense when our ancestors encountered new objects for the first time: "Is that woolly white thing going to attack me if I get closer to it?" After a few encounters it is deemed safe and there's no need to waste all that energy on tiptoeing past the sheep; unconscious and conscious attention can be directed elsewhere.

In one study Song and Schwarz tested reactions to different fonts by giving participants instructions for either cooking or performing an exercise in an easy- or hard-to-read font. They found that when the font was harder to read people assumed that the same behavior would take longer, be harder, and necessitate greater skill. We're so preoccupied with doing what's easiest that even a typeface can shape our response.[9]

There's also a fascinating leading principle with fluency. When something is primed by a related word or image that thing becomes more likeable. In experiments when people are shown the word "key" or "lock," they like a subsequent picture of a lock more than people who've been primed by an unrelated word such as "snow."[10] It would seem that when seeing one thing the brain opens up access to other related items just in case, and when that object appears the ease with which it can be accessed is interpreted as us liking that thing more.

But it doesn't just require a direct link between two items to trick our brains into liking what's easy or fluent. Labroo, Dhar, and Schwarz found that a highly familiar yet unconnected image on a wine label, such as a frog, increased liking for the product compared with a label without a distinctive and familiar image.[11]

Several years ago I was asked by a company whose sales were in decline to explore perceptions of its brand and food products. During the research I gave respondents a product to taste but didn't tell them anything about it. The response was overwhelmingly positive and the consensus was that the company would benefit enormously from launching the product; almost everyone I interviewed intended to buy it. However, the product had already been on the market for more than a year, in a clearly differentiated pack design, and the brand users I was interviewing had been taking their usual product off the shelf and ignoring the new one entirely.

The extent to which this preference for what's familiar can stretch is quite extraordinary. An analysis of share performance found that both in an artificial laboratory simulation and in real-life stock markets, shares with names (ticker codes) that were easier to say were predicted to perform better and actually did so![12]

Another dimension to this affection for the known emerges from the bizarre discovery that people are more likely to live in a town or have a job that has a link to their name, either through it sounding similar or by virtue of it beginning with the same letter.[13] American researchers Pelham, Mirenberg, and Jones attribute this irrational outcome to our capacity for implicit egotism, borne of our preference for things that are connected to ourselves. Ultimately, in real consumer situations (as opposed to research situations), people are attracted toward what's familiar and easiest to process mentally, rather than what's new.

Attempts to use market research as a forecasting tool are notoriously unreliable, and yet the practice continues. Sometimes this happens because companies have geared up their business on the basis that it works. For example, the research on the Pontiac Aztek didn't highlight the car's lack of appeal. Conversely, Chrysler's research on the PT Cruiser led to a dramatic underestimate of how many it would sell. On other occasions research continues to be used because accepting the alternative is inconvenient. Opinion polls give politicians and the media plenty of ammunition for debate, but nothing they would attach any importance to if they considered their hopeless inaccuracy when compared with the real data of election results (and that's after the polls have influenced the outcome of the result they're seeking to forecast).

Seeing into the future

When exploring something new in research, its appeal may be enhanced by the focalism of the research process and its risk-free novelty or, as Red Bull illustrated, devoid of the social context that will ultimately make it appealing. Futurology-style research also fails to take account of the fluency challenge facing whatever is being researched when it is encountered in the real world, where the familiarity of what we usually see and do takes over, resulting in the new product being either entirely overlooked or rejected. Just as Chapter 1 showed that we are poor witnesses to our own past behavior because of our inability to access the unconscious processes that drive so much of it, so it is when we attempt to predict our future. It's worth noting too that the issues I've described can be compounded when several new things are tested. Such exercises become implicitly comparative and inevitably something will be deemed "best." So what, if anything, can be done?

Understanding customers in the present and appreciating how they have changed in the past are valuable tools. Of course, given what I've discussed up to this point, I'm not advocating self-report and self-analysis-style market research informing about these issues. The challenge is to observe and interpret the behavior of your customers and place it in an appropriate historical context. In this sense, launching a new product is much like buying a present for someone. The better you know the person, the better you know how they've reacted in the past, the more likely you are to buy something they really appreciate, but there is always the possibility that you will miss the mark.

When looking to the future it is important to separate the stages of research that are actually concerned with future response from those that are gauging current behavior. It may be more convenient to discuss what consumers currently do and then introduce your "solution," but such a process is a recipe for inaccuracy. Depending on the nature of the problem and the style of research this can cause one of two issues. It risks constructing the problem and then presenting a logical conscious solution, in which case why wouldn't someone think it's a good idea? Or else it reinforces what people currently do, encouraging them to construct conscious reasons, and then offers them an alternative that requires them to devalue the rationale they've only just constructed!

Where future research is a question of "Will customers like this alternative version of something that exists if we offer it to them tomorrow?", the closer to the real-world context it can be placed the better. That may be through a large-scale trial, but at the very least a customer's real purchase mindset should be recreated and as much contextual information as physically possible provided to mirror the competing alternatives and aspects that will be unconsciously processed in reality. Naturally, the more artificial the test, the less weight should be attached to it in the overall decision-making process.

When future research is a question of the genuinely innovative, we must accept that consumers can't make those predictions any better than us, just because they might buy the product concerned. As Patrick Dixon, futurist and author of *Futurewise*, explained using his mother as an example in a speech to the leadership team of cellphone network MTN:

> *So we listen to our customers, we get close to them, listen to my mother please, but just don't believe what she says. We build an image of what her life is like, then using your techno-vision we build a vision, a future, that my mother may live in and we try to imagine how she will behave in that place.*[14]

When an initiative involves something genuinely new, the challenge is to forecast the future ourselves by estimating how the product itself and the marketing created to influence how people feel about it will affect the consumer landscape. The key issue then is not what research techniques can be devised, but how an organization can gear itself up so that it is equipped to test such innovations quickly and cost-effectively, roll them out with deference to the fact they may not succeed, and accept the financial pain and opportunity to learn when what are essentially entrepreneurial endeavors fail.

9

GAINING AN EDGE

Beyond market research

In the past 50 years market research has really become an unhelpful distraction to business. The implicit belief is that perfect judgments can be made each time a decision exists to be taken, so long as the right people are asked the right questions in the right way. Over this period many of the initiatives that the research process has informed have gone on to be successful, although I suspect often not for the reasons research thought they were. Such "successes" have been enough to justify the wishful thought that people usually know what they think and why they do what they do; a thought that most of us would prefer to believe is true of ourselves.

Market research is a relatively new invention. Before it occurred to someone that you could just ask people what they thought and what they wanted and do whatever they said, some other process was required. As long ago as the 1920s, Claude Hopkins wrote *Scientific Advertising*. In it he explained that expertise in advertising should be developed by learning the principles and proving them by repeated tests, comparing one way with another, and studying the results:

> *One ad is compared to another, one method with another. Headlines, settings, sizes, arguments and pictures are compared. To reduce the cost of results even one percent means much in some mail order advertising. One must know what is best.*
>
> *In lines where direct returns are impossible we compare one town with another. Scores of methods may be compared in this way, measured by cost of sales.*[1]

As the title of his book suggests, Hopkins believed in a scientific approach. But he did that because it gave him the license to suggest things that his clients thought were ridiculous and to show that his creativity, understanding of people, and belief in the benefits of advertising were justified. When he was presented with a dud soap brand called Palmolive, he recalled from his bible-studying days that olive oil had been used by the wealthy as a beauty treatment. His clients thought that his ad, depicting Cleopatra's skin being rubbed with oil, was bizarre, but he tested the campaign and it succeeded. Hopkins had invented beauty advertising.

What *we* can add to the process is an understanding of human psychology. This understanding is continually evolving, but it's important to recognize that people themselves are more or less a constant; it is the *context* that shifts. As Hopkins said:

> *Human nature is perpetual. In most respects, it is the same today as in the time of Caesar. So the principles of psychology are fixed and enduring.*

Ultimately, success will be determined not by how thoroughly organizations research their customers, but by how astutely they are able to understand the response to what they are currently doing and how quickly they can evaluate and implement alternatives. The classic case of Avis Rent a Car's "We Try Harder" campaign is an example that encapsulates all of the elements of the research dilemma. The campaign acknowledged the company's number two position in the market and people in focus groups hated it, but the confidence of agency chief Bill Bernbach and willingness of Avis CEO Robert Townshend to try it led to the company challenging Hertz for the number one position for the first time. Two years later Avis dropped the campaign: once people had tried Avis they didn't always like what they experienced. Hertz counter-attacked with a campaign that told customers it was number one for a reason (a powerful social proof message). As one commentator put it, "People didn't care how hard Avis tried, they only cared how effective Avis was." It didn't help that, while the slogan became something of a cultural sensation, comedians picked

up on the campaign and jokes about "number twos" became associated with Avis.

So in one short period, during which the market share of the
two companies shifted by as much as 10 percentage points, research
was unable to predict how people would respond to the campaign
in reality, nor that the campaign would ultimately be unsuccessful
because of a competitor's response, nor the greater impact on customers' perceptions when operational mistakes happened after people had been so sensitized to the company's customer service
efforts. Everybody was right, everybody was wrong.

The AFECT criteria:
How much faith can you have in any consumer insight?

One of my reasons for writing this book is that consumer research
reaches and affects so many people in business. Whether it is the
informal feedback solicited by someone with a small business or
the employee of a larger company sitting in a research debrief, it
can be difficult to reconcile the feeling that what you're hearing
isn't right with the fact that an apparently well-intentioned market
researcher has gathered the information in an established and professional manner from people who you believe are your customers.
Hopefully, I will have explained this lack of congruence for both
groups.

However, the desire for reassurance is such that undoubtedly
readers of this book will still find themselves in situations where
they or their organization still want something to lessen the feeling
of risk and responsibility in decisions where trials aren't possible.
How confident should you be that what you're hearing in a
research debrief is something you should take to heart and act on?
When should you make a stand for the feeling you have that an
alternative course of action is preferable to the one recommended
by the research agency?

Traditionally, the issue of confidence in research findings has
been the domain of statistics. As I said in the introduction, I have
no issue with statistical methods; in my view they are pure

concepts that are no less valid than basic arithmetic. Granted, they are open to abuse. Just as language can be used selectively so that the truth isn't told but nor is a lie, the selective application of statistical methods is rife with the potential to mislead. But in consumer research the fundamental issue really has nothing to do with the likelihood that if the survey were repeated the same answer would be obtained most of the time, give or take a few percentage points each way. The real question is whether the process has a chance of soliciting reliable information in the first place. As a result, the old chestnut of asking "How many people did we ask?" is not particularly relevant; at the very least, it should be the last basis for doubting the data rather than the first (and only) one.

So when that sinking feeling strikes you in a research debrief, how are you to decide whether it's because your preconceived notions have been legitimately confounded by consumers, or because the research process is flawed? Is it you or the researcher who's bad at their job?

Fortunately, by evaluating five aspects of the research process behind the "insights" being offered, you can gauge how much faith you should have in the conclusions. Consideration of the AFECT criteria will show how confident you can be about what research is telling you.

1 **A**FECT: Analysis of behavioral data

The first, and most important, question to consider is whether what you are being asked to believe is an analysis of consumer behavior or not. Is it information about what consumers do (or have done), or is it consumers' opinions about themselves? Chapters 1, 3, 4, and 7 of this book provide copious examples of why, if it's the latter, you have strong grounds for skepticism.

As I hope I've demonstrated, sales data and behavioral observation should inspire the most confidence. Where it is impossible to gather such data, ensuring that the research is derived from a behavioral focus – rather than from soliciting conscious attitudes and feelings – offers the best prospect of identifying unconscious associations and emotions. The alternative of conscious introspection normally required of the research interview process is best avoided. Even when the nature of a project demands that the research process looks into the future, I would argue that the only reliable insights will come from an analysis of current consumer behavior. Recognizing that the futurology required by many marketing projects is divorced from the process of consumer investigation is, at least, more honest, as well as affording the opportunity to learn from one's mistakes.

2 AFECT: Frame of mind

Where consumer evidence is gathered covertly from observing the relevant retail environment, the consumer mindset takes care of itself. However, when research is conducted overtly or remotely from the consumer environment, it is more likely that the mindset of the respondent will be at odds with the real one than that it will happen to coincide with it.

Where research has been conducted without reference to the way consumers behave when interacting with the product, service, or communication, it should merit no greater confidence than were it to have been obtained by interviewing an irrelevant target audience. When there is evidence that the research has encouraged an artificial mindset – for instance by making an experience that is usually unconscious and fun, conscious and analytical, or one that is a source of anxiety, calm and considered – it should merit no greater confidence than if it had asked questions about the wrong subject!

3 AFECT: Environment

Another question to consider is the context of the research. If behavioral data isn't available, at least research conducted in the appropriate consumer environment will have the contextual influences present. Just as importantly, it won't have an entirely different set of environmental influences, created by virtue of the research having taken place elsewhere.

In the case of products, have the price, packaging, and competing products been included? Have unrelated products that would normally be available around the subject of the research been present? The more research becomes a process scrutinizing one aspect of the total consumer experience, the less likely it is to be able to reflect reality and real consumer responses.

4 AFE**C**T: Covert study

Whatever the basis for the information, behavioral or otherwise, it is important to consider how apparent the focus of the research was to the consumers concerned. Where the subject of research *is* apparent, it dramatically increases the likelihood of influencing the response obtained. Putting the subject matter of research into the path of respondents creates a heightened sense of self-awareness that is likely to change how people behave.

While concealing the specific target of research among other alternatives is beneficial, for example testing alternative packaging designs from different brands, it is far better to conceal the nature of the research entirely by promoting it as being about something else altogether. For example, you could invite people to take part in a general discussion about newspapers while testing reactions to new packaging for a drink by having a selection of the products available, inviting people back the following day, and seeing if they select the same product and, if so, how quickly.

5 AFE**CT**: Timeframe

Tempting as it is to believe that a detailed, in-depth, considered response is more dependable than a brief reaction, a process that turns a consumer experience that takes place in just a few seconds into a 90-minute discussion or 10-minute question-and-answer session should not persuade you. On the contrary, any time you believe the unconscious mind is involved, a quick response (that is, the one that takes place in the first second or so) is much more dependable. Consumer reality should determine the research process, not the amount of justification felt to be required.

The AFECT criteria provide a means of gauging the extent to which consumer research findings are an artificial by-product of the research process or an accurate reflection of consumer reality. They are a good tool to use when considering if an investment in research is likely to be beneficial.

I have just completed a project testing new in-store communication and price tickets. My client had developed fresh information about how various products could make life easier for customers and was keen to learn the extent to which they helped people choose the right product for them. Many companies would have tested the communication in depth interviews or focus groups, and asked target consumers to discuss how useful they thought the information was; this approach would even have afforded the option of testing alternatives. For a moment let's assume this approach was used. How reliable might the research be?

A *Would it be an analysis of behavioral data?* No.

F *Would consumers be in a realistic frame of mind?* It is possible to get consumers into a realistic mindset, but most research of this type invites either a critical (Parent ego state) or balanced rational (Adult) mindset through the nature of the questioning exchange and the moderator's style.

E *How real would the environment (or context) be?* It would be extremely difficult (and expensive) to recreate the store environment.

C *Would the focus of the research be covert?* No, it would be overt.

T *Would the timeframe given for response match the timeframe consumers would usually use?* Almost certainly not. The length of the interview would be considerably longer than the time it took to read the sign, but it might be possible to record an initial reaction and use it to measure the impact of the communication (although what would the rest of the interview be spent doing?).

I would suggest that such an approach should inspire a very low level of "psychological confidence." Consumers would be engaging artificially with the communication and the risk of their processing it in a way other than that in which they normally would is considerable. Not least, as you will see in a moment, this approach entirely disregards the most critical component of all.

Instead of conducting an artificial piece of research, my client opted to conduct a live trial and asked me to help evaluate the impact of the new communication. During the day I spent watching customers, it became apparent that no one shopping in the store looked at the new communication for more than a fraction of a second – nowhere near long enough to process consciously what their eyes were scanning. I deduced that they were unconsciously filtering out what was there, regarding it as irrelevant, and consequently it would have no opportunity to help them select a product. To confirm this, I intercepted customers and, with their back to the display, asked them what was on the communication. Some people guessed incorrectly (providing a suggestion of what their unconscious might have been hoping to see), some couldn't recall anything, and some were totally unaware of the sign. I could advise my client with complete certainty that there was no point in pursuing the communication as intended and provide some clues as to what might work better based on what customers had inadvertently revealed when guessing.

A *Was it an analysis of behavioral data?* Yes.

F *Were consumers in a realistic frame of mind?* Yes, each customer's mindset was purely a by-product of his or her own experience.

E *How real was the environment?* The environment was completely authentic.

C *Was the focus of the research covert?* Yes.

T *Did the timeframe given for response match the timeframe consumers would usually use?* Yes, it was determined by consumers themselves (and measurable in tenths of a second).

My clients could have complete confidence in the accuracy of what I was reporting. Even though only one store was used in the test, the results were so clear-cut that any sales variations could confidently be attributed to external factors.

To illustrate this qualitative scale further, it is interesting to compare how well various hypothetical examples of consumer research perform. At one extreme, consider a live trial of a new pack design. A small run of sample packs are produced and stocked in a suitably typical retail outlet, and success is gauged via sales, covert behavioral observation of consumers buying the product (e.g., time spent considering, whether the new pack is touched or not, and so on), and possibly supplemented by exit interviews to confirm or clarify what's been observed, and to identify what was and wasn't influential.

A *Is it an analysis of behavioral data?* Yes.
F *Were consumers in the right frame of mind?* Each customer's mindset was purely a by-product of his or her own experience, both prior to and during the interaction with the store, fixture, and product.
E *How real was the environment?* The only element changed was the substitution of the new pack being tested.
C *Was the focus of the research covert?* Yes.
T *Did the timeframe given for response match the timeframe consumers would usually use?* Yes. Consumers determined how long they spent at the fixture without being aware that they were involved in a research process of any kind.

Given that the research process has stayed out of the consumer experience, one can feel very confident about the likely performance of the new pack in the market as a whole. If the pack has performed poorly (in contrast with the immediate prior sales of the existing pack in the same store and a separate control store selling the original pack over the time of the test), there will be evidence of whether this is because it was selected and rejected from the behavioral observation, an understanding of whether this was conscious or unconscious from the subsequent interview, and, if it was conscious, the reasons for it. Granted, consumers won't be providing the brief for the redesign, but unless they provided the brief for the original design, what's happened to turn them into experts all of a sudden?

Alternatively, the manufacturer decides to solicit consumer opinion through an internet survey. An online research company sends an email out to thousands of people who have subscribed, asking them to complete a short survey in exchange for payment or entry into a prize draw for a few thousand pounds. Participants sit at their computer and answer a series of questions about how they buy motor oil, before being shown some pack designs to rate, along with a 500-word summary of the product's positioning, and are then asked to rate some statements about their attitude to the product.

A *Is it an analysis of behavioral data?* No.

F *Were consumers in the right frame of mind?* Probably not. Respondents are sitting in front of their computers, probably at home, probably in the evening, probably in the midst of internet-related leisure activity. They are not taking part in the survey because they need motor oil. The experience is one of heightened consciousness, answering questions on a computer in a way that has far more in common with taking a test than it does the purchase experience concerned.

E *How real was the environment?* Unless most sales happen online, and even then unless products are purchased after a detailed question-and-answer session, one would have to say that the environment has no similarity to the retail one in which purchase decisions will actually be made.

C *Was the focus of the research covert?* No, it was overt. From the outset respondents have been told that they are taking part in a survey on motor oil. The nature of the questionnaire makes it impossible for them to be under any illusion about what is being researched.

T *Did the timeframe given for response match the timeframe consumers would usually use?* No. Respondents are reading statements and summaries and their reaction to the pack design is the result of a relatively long run-up of questions relating to the purchase of motor oil.

While this internet survey will produce a wealth of data relatively inexpensively, there is no reason to feel confident that the data will reflect the way in which consumers will respond when encountering the product for real. Since none of the six conditions has been met, there is a very high likelihood that consumers have presented how they would like to believe they make decisions, and what they think would make a product appealing, but there is no way of knowing how much conscious invention has taken place. Rather, given the shift in mindset and the nature of the questions, there are considerable grounds to ignore the results entirely.

As a further alternative approach, say the manufacturer is unable to secure the cooperation of a retailer, or isn't prepared to make the investment in producing a limited run of the new packs, and wants to obtain a consumer perspective before taking one of the designs it has developed further. After observing customers in-store to identify the typical behavior and mindset of a motor oil consumer, people who purchase motor oil are recruited for individual interviews (although that product is concealed among many other products they are asked about). Mock displays are created (either virtually or physically) to simulate visually as much of the store as possible, within which the new design is substituted. Each respondent is directed into the appropriate frame of mind and asked to make a number of product purchases from the simulated display, including one for motor oil, and told that they will be asked to pay for their product, which they'll receive at the end of the process. Their behavior, any questions they ask, and the choices they make are analyzed. Subsequently questions may be asked to confirm or clarify the choices made, before their money is returned to them.

A *Is it an analysis of behavioral data?* Partially. Behavior has been observed and then simulated, rather than attitudes or opinions solicited.

F *Were consumers in a realistic frame of mind?* Yes. Observation was used to identify customers' mindset, and this mindset was recreated in the simulated shopping experience.

E *How real was the environment?* It was a simulation. Some of the contextual information was available, but the environment was different.

C *Was the focus of the research covert?* Primarily covert. The product of interest wasn't identified and was concealed with several other products.

T *Did the timeframe given for response match the timeframe consumers would usually use?* Yes. Respondents are making a purchase decision rather than answering a series of questions.

In this case the research has met three of the conditions and partially met the other two. While not providing the reassurance of a live test, it does take account of the role of the unconscious and the potential impact of contextual elements by simulating a purchase. By including price information and requiring respondents to make a physical payment, it also does all it can to make the decision as risk sensitive as it would be in reality. Note, too, that it has avoided inviting an artificial conscious analysis of the new product by isolating it, not making it the overt focus of the experience, and not asking questions that can change how and what people think.

A final check, which can be used to assess the likelihood that information obtained from consumers is reliable, is whether the learning is congruent with that from the experiments conducted by consumer and social psychologists. Is it in line with learning about how the unconscious drives responses, or with research on how people are influenced? If the answer is yes, the research has at the very least coincided with behavioral traits identified independently elsewhere.

Value for money

It might surprise you to hear that I don't think traditional "asking people what they want and listening to their answers" research is entirely futile. My issue is with research that, duplicitously or otherwise, is relied on to provide an ultimately unjustifiable sense of reassurance about a decision that is being taken or, worse still, to inform an organization's strategy. Every now and then it is inevitable that someone will, in response to a question, say something that triggers a good idea, constructive change, or worthwhile action. But the operative word is *someone*. If human beings were routinely capable of such accurate introspection, psychoanalysts could be replaced by a two-line computer program that asked patients what their problem was and told them to do whatever they thought best to resolve it. Such sparks of astute observation or innovation are not and cannot be a dependable consequence of a conscious interviewing process, and so the only benefit of asking more people is an increased chance of encountering one person who does have such insight. Of course, whether a person's comment *is* valuable or not is a qualitative judgment; its value is in triggering an association or reinforcing a prejudice in the mind of the decision maker.

While asking one question is inherently problematic, asking several makes it much more likely that the questioning process will influence the answers obtained, thus the case for large-scale, long-interview market research is extremely dubious. And yet this is exactly how the market research industry has typically defined the value of its offer.

When considered in this way, the approach and value of such research are brought into focus. Is it really necessary to speak to a large number of people? Is a "trained" moderator required to ask the questions? Is a detailed report of what everyone who was interviewed said likely to be helpful? Most importantly of all, how much should be spent on such a process? Wouldn't it be better for whoever is tasked with the decision to put themselves among the people of interest to them and let unconscious and conscious stimuli, allied to whatever expertise has put them in the decision-making position they occupy, trigger in them the feeling of what they should do?

Skilled observation, particularly where it brings an informed understanding of consumer psychology, can provide genuine insights into how and why people are behaving as they do and what might be done to influence them. However, just as a mechanic is most useful if he can listen to your car and diagnose its fault rather than taking the entire vehicle to bits to inspect each part, the value of such a service is not in its scale but in its ability to find the problems and provide appropriate solutions.

Gaining a competitive edge

In the future, the companies that gain an edge over their competitors will be those that, intuitively or through application, best understand the complex interplay that exists between their customers' unconscious and conscious minds. The understanding that is emerging from social psychology and neuroscience provides the insights that help explain why customers behave as they do, and why what seems logical or is endorsed by customers in an abstract context may not succeed in reality.

Scientific understanding about how the brain works is developing swiftly, but we are a long way off being able to read minds or predict what people will choose to do with accuracy. Designers have always known it is better to create an attractive retail space to sell products. Comprehending how apparently peripheral elements such as color, smell, and texture can dramatically shift how products are perceived helps bring some scientific knowledge to this process.

With the impact of the associative nature of the human mind and the role of unconscious filtering becoming better understood, there is an opportunity for organizations to get more in tune with their customers and be more effective at marketing to them. Historically, marketing has dealt in terms of consumer "needs," whereas what matters more when it comes to consumer behavior is how unconscious associations are managed, unconscious fears overcome, and uncomfortable confusion avoided.

The nature of unconscious misattribution, whereby a feeling created by one thing is projected onto another, is such that nothing may in fact be something. From studying the way in which people are influenced it is easy to see how, very often, success is achieved without any tangible, consciously appraisable benefit. A few years ago I was involved in a product launch for a new pizza for Pizza Hut. The concept that had been developed was for a product with larger toppings: the meat pieces were going to be chunkier, the vegetables more thickly sliced, and the more attractive red onion would replace white. The concept products were prepared and presented to a group of senior managers and directors and everyone agreed that the resulting pizza looked more appetizing. Over the next few weeks the product development team went to work on sourcing the necessary ingredients and establishing the final cost of the product.

When the product was presented to the board for approval along with the cost, the chief executive became nervous. The new ingredients were significantly more expensive and there was no plan to increase the price of the pizza. The members of the product team were sent away to see what they could do. Following a series of meetings where revised products with cheaper ingredients were presented and discussed, the board eventually reached a point where it was comfortable with launching the product. Unfortunately, by this stage as the launch deadline loomed, what little objectivity might have been present at the beginning of the process was gone, and the toppings had been reduced so much that, had anyone thought to put the existing version alongside the new one, they would have seen that you would have needed a micrometer to spot the difference in topping dimensions.

The launch went ahead, and the company announced its "new" product to the nation. Within a few days of the launch, several of us were called to a crisis meeting with the chief executive. Conveniently forgetting his involvement in the move to reduce the cost of the toppings, he demanded to know why the restaurant managers were saying that the new pizza looked no different from its predecessor.

If the company *had* conducted research in its standard comparative way, it is hard to imagine that it could have concluded anything *but* that the cost-managed "new" pizza was the same as the current one. In this situation, it would almost certainly not have launched the product. However, excited by celebrity-based advertising and promotional activity, people wanted to buy it and the launch was a success. The company had inadvertently conducted a successful live trial of an initiative that research would have rejected.

Developing cost-effective yet meaningful live tests should be a much higher priority than reaching for the researcher's clipboard or convening a focus group, and it demands an appreciation of the subtle elements that often influence consumer behavior. Many of the most interesting experiments in social psychology utilize a test-and-control approach whereby, unbeknown to the participants, a variable is altered and participants' reactions are observed. Through this kind of approach it is possible to identify, for example, that a simple change in the wording of a sign can dramatically alter the proportion of people who conform to a request, be it to keep a doctor's appointment or to reuse their hotel bath towel, or that a well-phrased apology can have a more powerful impact on how customers feel about being let down than putting money in their hand.[2]

One business that has very successfully embraced the benefits of leveraging live data is the world's biggest fashion retailer, Inditex (which owns brands including Zara, Bershka, and Massimo Dutti). It carefully monitors sales of new lines and captures unsolicited feedback from its stores, to the extent that around half of its clothing collections evolve and adapt during each season. In essence, every day of the business is a live test in more than 4,000 stores across 73 countries and the company is obsessive about learning from every moment: not just which garments are selling, but which colors, sizes, and shapes. With its marketing, design, and manufacturing tuned to respond and adapt to the feedback it captures, successful ranges can be continued, promoted more prominently, and expanded, and those that aren't working can be swiftly withdrawn and replaced without the burden of excessive stock. In addition to the unparalleled speed of feedback that this approach provides, it also engages employees as experts in their business of connecting with customers, rather than outsourcing this role to market research organizations. It's easy to understand why Inditex's chief operating officer believes that the store managers appreciate being able to contribute in this way and perform better as a consequence.[3]

We are at the dawn of an exciting time for understanding consumers. Developments in social psychology, neural imaging, and a number of technologies that covertly track the movements of shoppers are providing new insights into what people do and why. But technology will also tempt people into gathering customers' opinions swiftly at the expense of accuracy, either because it appeals to our vain notion of conscious will, or because it panders to a desire to place convenience above accuracy.

Ultimately, the prize for organizations that are willing to remove their dependency on traditional approaches to market research is considerable. By recognizing that consumers aren't well placed to tell us how they do or will behave, and developing alternative approaches to evaluating and testing, we can place consumers much closer to the "heart of a business" than they are at present. The benefit of divorcing oneself from superstition is the opportunity to take responsibility for one's own success and to learn the lessons from failures. Just as you got promoted not because of the "current planetary energy at play" but because you did something well, a new product deserves to be launched not because consumers approved it in focus groups, but because someone saw the opportunity for it.

Of course, where research is used as a crutch to give a sense of risk minimization (however unfounded), moving ahead without it may not feel comfortable. Nevertheless, as I have explained, it is not a question of all or nothing; rather, it's a matter of reappraising what can and can't be validated with consumers and recognizing that the key to their "thoughts" lies in studying what they actually *do*, not what they say when they're invited to think about it.

Arguably, no company illustrates the benefit of this approach more than Apple, which has recognized the important distinction between needing to be able to connect with and relate to your customers and the futility of attempting to consolidate these people into representative data. Few could doubt Apple's ability to create products that really resonate with consumers although, as Steve Jobs told *Fortune*, "We do no market research." It is a company that employs people who are just like the people they want to sell to, and they develop the products and services that they find really exciting themselves, then take them to market with the enthusiasm and confidence they genuinely feel for what they have created.[4]

EPILOGUE

Shortly before this book went to press, my publisher directed my attention to a survey that had been distributed within the publishing world. A US book advertising agency had commissioned research of what it erroneously described as "book buying behavior."[1] In fact the study consisted of responses to a questionnaire distributed online. The survey's results were primed with satisfying numerological reassurance: with over 5,500 responses the survey "validation" stated that the data had a 1.6 percentage point margin of error at the 95% probability threshold. With the sample weighted to reflect the adult US population as a whole, the book industry recipients could feel reassured that what the company had learned from the research was true.

However, using the AFECT criteria that I described in the last chapter to evaluate the results, they are worthless. Despite the title's claim, the survey isn't an analysis of behavioral data, it comprises people's claimed preferences and self-reported reading and purchase behavior.

No attempt was made to identify the frame of mind a book buyer was in, or rather frames of mind, since no doubt different genres and different start points invoke different attitudes to purchasing. I imagine the student told he should buy a book for his course will be thinking very differently from the person who is browsing at the airport and happens upon something of great interest.

The environment of the survey was the abstract world of the computer questionnaire: a screen filled with words and check boxes and devoid of even the limited subliminally persuasive context that online book retailers are able to deploy.

The research was entirely overt: anyone completing the questionnaire would be aware what the survey was seeking to learn and would also be mindful of how they wanted themselves to be perceived by anyone considering their responses. Moreover, the invitation to take part would have explained that the questionnaire was about book buying. Those least interested in books would, in all likelihood, be least interested in participating.

Lastly, the time involved in the consideration process is determined by the style of the questionnaire and the way people react to its questions. With no attempt having been made to identify a book-buying consideration process, we can only speculate about whether the speed of thought applied is consistent.

Using the AFECT criteria, the survey isn't worth a bean. But even without that analysis, only a moderate dose of research skepticism is required to see that it was a worthless exercise.

Independent book stores were rated as the favorite place to shop for books, despite them having just 10% of book sales by revenue. Given that such stores tend to be more expensive than their online and supermarket competitors, their share of volume is almost certainly even lower. The company that commissioned the research was so surprised by this result that it ran the survey (in exactly the same way) for a second time; it got the same result. However, rather than draw the conclusion that people consistently say things that aren't reflected in their behavior, something that would undermine the entire survey, it decided that this meant independent book retailers had a market share that was "lower than their mind share."

In another misguided quantification of the irrelevant, the survey investigated what people believed shaped their purchase behavior by asking which "marketing awareness" factors were important. Given the evident capacity people have to be influenced outside of conscious awareness (detailed in Chapter 1), there is simply no way in which the responses to a prompted list of traditional marketing tools can produce an accurate assessment of what has really shaped their purchase choices.

The results of the question on online marketing awareness factors would have us believe that around one third of book buyers reference authors' websites and blogs. I sincerely doubt that the web traffic of these sites would show hits at a rate equivalent to one third of book sales, and I also doubt that much of this traffic occurs prior to purchase. In any event, it would be far better to check this true behavioral statistic across a random sample of authors, than to invest money in this area on the basis of such generalized claims from a survey that has already proven itself inaccurate.

The survey also indulged in some futile futurology on the subject of ereaders and ebooks: were people going to buy one, how many books would they buy, did they want the two formats bundled together, how much would they pay for ebooks? On the day the results to these questions arrived in my publisher's inbox, Steve Jobs was standing in front of a media audience in San Francisco unveiling Apple's new iPad. I hope that traditional books survive, but when the company's iBooks store is launched the parallels between music and literature will be obvious. The battle between fidelity and convenience will be waged and it would be a brave publisher who didn't gear up for a shift in the market.

So an apparently valid survey can be leveraged for self-interest and self-delusion, leaving publishers to scratch their heads when their sales decline, their campaign to support independent book stores falls flat, and they lose market share to people in their bedrooms who can readily make an electronic book feel like one that has been through the valuable screening and editing process that publishers provide. Alternatively, publishers can look at how the real behavioral numbers are shifting and consider what they add to the process of bringing a book to market. They could start lobbying Apple to delineate the homespun from the established. At the very least, they can work to ensure that iBooks displays information that differentiates the scale of a book's publisher. They could start building the prominence of their own brand to ensure it becomes an influential factor for book buyers. They could also consider how they might transform their own, mostly outdated, websites into places readers would want to visit and perhaps even buy from.

One thing is certain: It is only by distinguishing between the bogus consumer.ology and genuine insights into consumer behavior that any organization is going to improve its chances of being successful in the future.

NOTES

Overture

1. www.pulsetoday.co.uk/story.asp?storycode=4116359.
2. Sporting Superstitions: www.24.com/sport/?p=SportArticle&i=482871.
3. Brown, D. (2007) *Tricks of the Mind*, London: Channel 4 Books, pp 292–3.
4. Rowlands, M. (2008) *The Philosopher and the Wolf: Lessons from the Wild on Love, Death and Happiness*, London: Granta Books. I don't presume to have done justice to Mark Rowlands' wonderful book with this brief distillation of its conclusions.
5. LeDoux, J. (1998) *The Emotional Brain*, London: Phoenix, p. 267.
6. Fine, C. (2007) *A Mind of its Own: How Your Brain Distorts and Deceives*, London: Icon Books.
7. Gladwell, M. (2006) *Blink: The Power of Thinking Without Thinking*, Harmondsworth: Penguin, pp 16–17.

Chapter 1

1. Gladwell, M. (2006) *Blink: The Power of Thinking without Thinking*, Harmondsworth: Penguin.
2. Pendergrast, M. (2000) *For God, Country and Coca-Cola: The Unauthorized History of the World's Most Popular Soft Drink and the Company that Makes It*, New York: Basic Books.
3. University of Toronto (2009) Don't I know you? How cues and context kick-start memory recall, *ScienceDaily*, December 12.
4. I suspect that, were it not for our conversation, within a few days of buying the washing machine the woman would have claimed that she bought the product because of the brand's outright reliability, and not because she had no other basis for purchase and was confused by the choice available.
5. Hogan, K. (2004) *The Science of Influence: How to Get Anyone to Say Yes in 8 Minutes or Less!*, Chichester: John Wiley.
6. www.businessweek.com/smallbiz/content/mar2010/sb20100312_705320.htm.
7. Martin, J. (1995) Managing: Ideas and solutions, *Fortune*, 131(8): 121.
8. Li, W., Moallem, I., Paller, K.A. & Gottfried, J.A. (2007) Subliminal smells can guide social preferences, *Psychological Science*, 18(12): 1044–9.
9. www.nytimes.com/2007/09/09/realestate/keymagazine/909SCENTtxt.html?_r=1&pagewanted=5&ref=keymagazine.
10. Bahrami, B., Lavie, N. & Rees, G. (2007) Attentional load modulates responses of human primary visual cortex to invisible stimuli, *Current Biology*, March.
11. Bargh, J. A. & Pietromonaco, P. (1982) Automatic information processing and social perception: The influence of trait information presented outside of conscious awareness on impression formation, *Journal of Personality and Social Psychology*, 43: 437–449.
12. Draine, S. & Greenwald, A. (1999) Replicable unconscious semantic priming, *Journal of Experimental Social Psychology: General*, 127: 286–303, taken from Wilson, T. (2002) *Strangers to Ourselves: Discovering the Adaptive Unconscious*, Boston, MA: Belknap Press.

13 Plassmann, H., O'Doherty, J., Shiv, B., & Rangel, A. (2008) Marketing actions can modulate neural representations of experienced pleasantness, *Proceedings of the National Academy of Sciences*, 105(3).

14 www.sciencedaily.com/releases/2007/08/070806104111.htm, Aug 11 2007, research by Cornell University.

15 Moll, A. (1889) *Hypnotism*, New York: Scribner's.

16 Wilson & Nesbitt, taken from Wilson, *op. cit.*

17 Nisbett & Wilson, taken from Wilson, *op. cit.*

18 Wegner, D.M. (2003) *The Illusion of Conscious Will*, Cambridge, MA: MIT Press.

19 Soon, C.S., Brass, M., Heinze, H.-J., & Haynes, J.-D. (2008) Unconscious determinants of free decisions in the human brain, *Nature Neuroscience*, April 13.

20 Damasio, A. (2000) *The Feeling of What Happens: Body, Emotion and the Making of Consciousness*, London: Vintage.

21 www.widerfunnel.com/proof/case-studies/babyage-com-e-commerce-retailer-lifts-sales-conversion-rate-by-22-with-conversion-rate-optimization.

22 www.widerfunnel.com/proof/case-studies/sytropin-a-nutritional-supplement-sold-online-realizes-a-50-uplift-in-sales-conversions.

23 Bechara, A., Damasio, H., Tranel, D., & Damasio, A.R. (1997) Deciding advantageously before knowing the advantageous strategy, *Science*, 28 February, 275(5304): 1293–5.

24 Cooper, R.G., Edgett, S.J., & Kleinschmidt, E.J. (2004) Benchmarking best NPD practices – I, *Research Technology Management*, 47(1): 31–43.

Chapter 2

1 Pendergrast, *op. cit.*

2 Underhill, P. (1999) *Why We Buy: The Science of Shopping*, London: Orion Business, p. 210.

3 Lakhani, D. (2008) *Subliminal Persuasion: Influence and Marketing Secrets They Don't Want You to Know*, Chichester: John Wiley.

4 The title of Mark Pendergrast's chapter on the story of New Coke in his book, *op. cit.*

5 Kahneman & Tversky (1984) taken from Hogan, *op. cit.*

6 Perfect, T.J. & Askew, C. (1994) Print adverts: Not remembered but memorable, *Applied Cognitive Psychology*, 8.

7 Read Montague, P., McClure, S., Li, J., Cypert, K., & Montague, L. (2004) Neural correlates of behavioural preference for culturally familiar drinks, *Neuron*, 44(Oct.): 379–87.

8 Hogan, K. (2004) *The Science of Influence: How to Get Anyone to Say Yes in 8 Minutes or Less!*, Chichester: John Wiley, p153.

9 Pendergrast, *op. cit.*

10 http://news.bbc.co.uk/1/hi/health/1368912.stm.

11 Alter, A. L. & Oppenheimer, D. M. (2006) Predicting short-term stock fluctuations by using processing fluency, *Proceedings of the National Academy of Sciences*, 103: 9369–72.

12 Treiman, R., Kessler, B., & Bourassa, D. (2001) Children's own names influence their spelling, *Applied Psycholinguistics*, 22: 555–70.

13 www.widerfunnel.com/proof/case-studies/widerfunnel-increases-booking-conversion-rate-for-extra-space-storage-by-10-percent.

14 Blackmore, S. (1999) *The Meme Machine*, Oxford: Oxford University Press, p. 3.

15 Latane, B. & Darley, J.M. (1968) Group inhibition of bystander intervention in emergencies, *Journal of Personality and Social Psychology*, 10(3): 215–21; Latane, B. & Darley, J. (1969) Bystander "apathy," *American Scientist*, 57: 244–68.

16 Goldstein, N., Martin, S., & Cialdini, R. (2007) *Yes! 50 Secrets from the Science of Persuasion*, London: Profile.

17 Duhachek, A., Shuoyang, Z., & Krishnan, H.S. (2007) Anticipated group interaction: Coping with valence asymmetries in attitude shift, *Journal of Consumer Research*, 34(3): 395–405.

18 Hogan, *op. cit.*

19 *Ibid.*

20 Delgado, M.R., Frank, R.H., & Phelps, E.A. (2005) Perceptions of moral character modulate the neural systems of reward during the trust game, *Nature Neuroscience*, 8(11): 1611–18.

21 Ross, L., Lepper, M.R., & Hubbard, M. (1975) Perseverance in self-perception and social perception: Biased attributional processes in the debriefing paradigm, *Journal of Personality and Social Psychology*, 32: 880–92.

22 Pendergrast, *op. cit.*

Chapter 3

1   Respondents are taken to a room (hall) that has been set up for research, either simply for shelter, or where computers, video players, or other sources of stimulus (including mocked-up fixtures) can be used in the research process.

2   Areni, C. & Kim, D. (1993) The influence of background music on shopping behavior: Classical versus top-forty music in a wine store, *Advances in Consumer Research*, 336–40.

3   www.sfgate.com/cgi-bin/article.cgi?f=/c/a/2007/11/02/WI8oSAPJB.DTL.

4   Yalch, R. & Spangenberg, E. (2000) The effects of music in a retail setting on real and perceived shopping times, *Journal of Business Research*, 49: August; Timmerman, J. E. (1981) The effect of temperature, music and density on perception of crowding and shopping behaviour of consumers in a retail environment, *Dissertation Abstracts International* 42(3): 1293.

5   Milliman, R.E. (1982) Using background music to affect the behavior of supermarket shoppers, *Journal of Marketing*, 46(Summer): 86–91.

6   Summers, T. & Hebert, P. (2001) Shedding some light on store atmospherics influence of illumination on consumer behavior, *Journal of Business Research*, 54: 145–50.

7   Meyers-Levy, J. & Zhy, R. (2007) The influence of ceiling height: The effect of priming on the type of processing people use, *Journal of Consumer Research*, September.

8   Underhill, *op. cit.*, p. 102.

9   Bronner, F. & Kuijlen, K. (2007) The live or digital interviewer, *International Journal of Market Research*, 49(2).

10 Sparrow, N. (2006) Developing reliable on-line polls, *International Journal of Market Research*, 48(6).

11 De Pelsmacker, P., Geuens, M., & Anckaert P. (2002) Media context and advertising effectiveness: The role of context style, context quality and context-ad similarity, *Journal of Advertising*, 31(2): 49–61.

12 Nam, M. & Sternthal, B. (2008) The effects of a different category context on target brand evaluations, *Journal of Consumer Research*, December.

13 Yoon, S.-O. & Simonson, I. (2008) Choice set configuration as a determinant of preference attribution and strength, *Journal of Consumer Research*, 35(2): 324.

14 www.nytimes.com/1996/09/19/business/chief-of-mcdonald-s-defends-arch-deluxe-to-franchisees.html.

15 Haig, M. (2003) *Brand Failures: The Truth About the 100 Biggest Branding Mistakes of All Time*, London: Kogan Page.

16 Milgram, S. (1963) Behavioral study of obedience, *Journal of Abnormal & Social Psychology*, 67: 3771–8.

17 www.stanford.edu/dept/news/pr/97/970108prisonexp.html.

18 Gale Cengage (2001) Homosexuality, *1990s Lifestyles and Social Trends*, Gale Cengage.

19 Mattel Blooper: www.anecdotage.com.

20 Dutton, D. G. & Aron, A. P. (1974) Some evidence for heightened sexual attraction under conditions of high anxiety, *Journal of Personality and Social Psychology*, 30: 510–17.

21 I have been unable to establish if Peugeot conducted more formal market research on the 1007; it is perhaps not surprising that manufacturers and research agencies don't promote their work on products that fail. However, I would be shocked if it had not tested the concept through consumer research.

22 http://sitetuners.com/luggagepoint-case-study.html.

23 Nah, F. (2004) A study on tolerable waiting time: How long are Web users willing to wait?, *Behaviour & Information Technology*, 23(3): 153–63.

24 Google's Marissa Mayer: Speed wins, http://blogs.zdnet.com/BTL/?p=3925.

25 McKinsey Quarterly (2001) Getting prices right on the Web, cited in Constantinides, E. (2004) Influencing the online consumer's behavior: The Web experience, *Internet Research*, 14(2).

26 www.law.virginia.edu/html/librarysite/garrett_exonereedata.htm.

27 Hasel, L.E. & Kassin, S.M. (2009) On the presumption of evidentiary independence: Can confessions corrupt eyewitness identifications? *Psychological Science*, 20(1): 122.

28 Wegner, Vallacher, & Kelly, Identifications of the act of getting married, cited in Wegner, D.M. (2003) *The Illusion of Conscious Will*, Cambridge, MA: MIT Press.

29 *Telegraph Magazine*, 10 November 2007.

Chapter 4

1 Underhill, *op. cit.*, p. 171.

2 http://cmbi.bjmu.edu.cn/news/0607/110.htm; Wilson, T. (2002) *Strangers to Ourselves: Discovering the Adaptive Unconscious*, Cambridge, MA: Belknap Press.

3 University of Georgia (2008) Simple recipe for ad success: Just add art, *ScienceDaily*, Feb. 15.

4 Bem, D.J. (DATE?) *Self Perception Theory: Advances in Experimental Social Psychology*, Vol 6, New York: Academic Press.

5 Epley, N. & Dunning, D. (2000) Feeling "Holier than thou": Are self-serving assessments produced by errors in self or social prediction? *Journal of Personality and Social Psychology*, 79: 861–75.

6 Wilson, *op. cit.*, p84.

7 Underhill, *op. cit.*

8 Ohio State University (2009) You can look – but don't touch, *ScienceDaily*, January 12.

9   Greene, J. (2010) *Design Is How It Works: How the Smartest Companies Turn Products into Icons*, New York: Penguin.

10 Iyengar, S.S. & Lepper, M. (2000) When choice is demotivating: Can one desire too much of a good thing? *Journal of Personality and Social Psychology*, 79: 995–1006; Fasolo, B., Hertwig, R., Huber, M., & Ludwig, M. (2009) Size, entropy and density: What is the difference that makes makes the difference between small and large real-world assortments? *Psychology and Marketing*, 26(3); Broniarczyk, S.M., Hoyer, W.D., & McAlister, L. (1998) Consumers' perceptions of the assortment offered in a grocery category: The impact of item reduction, *Journal of Marketing Research*, 35(May): 166–76; Jessup, R.K., Veinott, E.S., Todd, P.M., & Busemeyer, J.R. (2009) Leaving the shop empty-handed: Testing explanations for the too-much-choice effect using decision field theory, *Psychology and Marketing*, 26(3): 299–320.

11 Kahneman, D. & Tversky, A. (1984) Choices, values and frames, *American Psychologist*, 39: 341–50.

12 Simonson, I. & Tversky, A. (1992) Choice in context: Tradeoff contrast and extremeness aversion, *Journal of Marketing Research*, 29(3): 281–95.

13 www.fourhourworkweek.com/blog/2009/08/12/google-website-optimizer-case-study/.

14 According to LeDoux, activation of the amygdala turns an experience into an emotional experience and this is much less well connected to the lateral prefrontal cortex (the area associated with consciousness) than other parts of the brain.

15 Darwin, C. cited in LeDoux, J. (1998) *The Emotional Brain: The Mysterious Underpinnings of Emotional Life*, New York: Simon and Schuster.

16 Stewart, I. & Joines, V. (1987) *TA Today: A New Introduction to Transactional Analysis*, Nottingham: Lifespace.

17 Thomas, L (1974) *The Lives of a Cell: Notes of a Biology Watcher*, London: Viking.

18 *British Medical Journal* (2007) Humor develops from aggression caused by male hormones, professor says, *ScienceDaily*, December 23.

19 www.clicktale.com.

Chapter 5

1   www.millennium.gov.uk/lottery/experience.html.

2   National Audit Office (2000) *The Millennium Dome: Report by The Comptroller and Auditor General*, HC 936 Session 1999–2000, 9 November.

3   M&C Saatchi, *Will 12 Million Visit the Dome?* www.culture.gov.uk/images/freedom_of_information/2975_3.pdf.

4   National Audit Office, *op. cit.*

5   www.guardian.co.uk/uk/1999/sep/17/fiachragibbons.

6   National Audit Office, *op. cit.*

7   As the name suggests, this is a research approach in which a researcher accompanies a consumer during their visit to the store and asks them questions about their experience as it happens.

8   Simons, D. & Chabris, C. (1999) Gorillas in our midst: Sustained inattentional blindness for dynamic events, *Perception*, 28: 1059–74.

9   Moore, D.W. (2008) *The Opinion Makers: An Insider Exposes the Truth Behind the Polls*, Lichfield: Beacon Press.

10 Wilson, T. & Schooler, J. (1991) Thinking too much: Introspection can reduce the quality of preferences and decisions, *Journal of Personality and Social Psychology*, 60: 181–92.

11 Tormala, Z.L. & Petty, R.E. (2007) Contextual contrast and perceived knowl-edge: Exploring the implications for persuasion, *Journal of Experimental Social Psychology*, 43: 17–30; Tormala, Z.L. & Clarkson, J.J. (2007) Assimilation and contrast in persuasion: The effects of source credibility in multiple message situations, *Personality and Social Psychology Bulletin*, April.

12 In some markets there is a degree of consumer protection to ensure that a product has been available elsewhere at the higher stated price for a defined period; however, while this provides a degree of reassurance, it's not to say that anyone bought the product from the branch of the store in Inverness that tried to sell it at the higher price!

13 Tversky. A. & Kahneman. D. (1974) Judgment under uncertainty, *Heuristics and Biases Science*, 185(4157, Sep. 27): 1124–31.

14 Wilson, T. D., Houston, C. E., Etling, K. M., & Brekke, N. (1996) A new look at anchoring effects: Basic anchoring and its antecedents, *Journal of Experimental Psychology: General*, 125: 387–402.

15 Moore, *op. cit.*

16 Market mapping involves establishing the relative position of competing products or brands, usually through asking respondents to place products into groups that they believe are similar; often the exercise is repeated to explore alternative dimensions of difference, for example people may separate out brands on the basis of perceived quality first, and when asked to do so a different way choose perceived healthiness. The criteria they employ to dif-ferentiate the brands are translated into axes, enabling the brands to be plot-ted in multiple dimensions.

17 Kim, K. & Meyers-Levy, J. (2008) Context effects in diverse-category brand environments: The influence of target product positioning and consumers' processing mind-set, *Journal of Consumer Research*, 34(April): 882–96.

18 Poncin, I., Pieters, R., & Ambaye, M. (2006) Cross advertisement affectivity: The influence of similarity between commercials and processing modes of consumers on advertising processing, *Journal of Business Research*, 59: 745–54.

19 Shen, H., Jiang, Y., & Adaval, R. (2010) Contrast and assimilation effects of processing fluency, *Journal of Consumer Research*, 36: 876–89.

20 www.nytimes.com/2001/01/09/health/in-weird-math-of-choices-6-choices-can-beat-600.html.

21 Kahneman and Tversky (1984) taken from Hogan, *op. cit.*

22 Hogan, *op. cit.*

23 Hogan, K., Lakhani, D., & May, G. (2007) *Selling: Powerful New Strategies for Sales Success*, Eagan, MN: Network 3000 Publishing.

24 McNeil, B. J., Pauker, S. G., Sox, H. C. Jr, & Tversky, A. (1982) On the elici-tation of preferences for alternative therapies, *New England Journal of Medicine*, 306: 1259–62.

25 Schwartz, B. (2004) *The Paradox of Choice: Why More is Less*, London: HarperCollins.

26 Moore, *op. cit.*

27 *Ibid.*

28 www.millennium-dome.com/news/news990318dometickets.htm.

29 Data quoted in National Audit Office, *op. cit.*, restated in population terms based on data from the Office for National Statistics quoted in a Government Actuaries Document (www.gad.gov.uk/Documents/Demography/Projections/2000-based_National_population_projections_reference_volume.pdf).

30 Small, D. A., Loewenstein, G., & Slovic, P. (2007) Sympathy and callousness: The impact of deliberative thought on donations to identifiable and statistical victims, *Organizational Behavior and Human Decision Processes*, 102: 143–53.

31 National Audit Office, *op. cit.*

32 Janis, I. L. & King, B. T. (1954) The influence of role-playing on opinion change, *Journal of Abnormal and Social Psychology*, 49: 211–18.

33 Shen, H. & Wyer, Jr., R.S. (2008) Procedural priming and consumer judgments: Effects on the impact of positively and negatively valenced information, *Journal of Consumer Research*, February.

34 I asked an American friend how he would characterize the E! channel, since I'd never watched it. He described it as "A gossip channel for morons who have nothing better to do than spend their life watching people follow Brittany Spears"; although he did concede he probably wasn't representative of the channel's target audience.

35 Duke University (2008) Logo can make you "think different," *ScienceDaily*, March 30.

36 Radiological Society of North America (2006) MRI shows brains respond better to name brands, *ScienceDaily*, November 30.

37 Haig, *op. cit.*

38 www.designweek.co.uk/news/dove-to-get-the-lynx-treatment/1121049.article.

39 www.american.com/archive/2007/july-august-magazine-contents/absolut-capitalism.

40 La Piere, R. T. (1934) Attitudes vs. actions, *Social Forces*, 13: 230–37.

41 Wright, M. & Klÿn, B. (1998) Environmental attitude behaviour correlations in 21 countries, *Journal of Empirical Generalisations in Marketing Science*, 3.

42 Berne, E. (1961) *Transactional Analysis in Psychotherapy: The Classic Handbook to Its Principles*, London: Souvenir Press; Berne, E. (1972) *What Do You Say After You Say Hello?*, London: Corgi Books; Stewart, I. & Jones, V. (1987) *TA Today: A New Introduction to Transactional Analysis*, Nottingham: Lifespace.

43 Technically McEnroe went into a Child in the Parent mode, based on the second-order structural model of TA.

44 If you exclude the Parentally dismissive "No thanks" when the clipboarded woman approaches the typical would-be respondent going about his high street shopping on a Saturday morning!

45 Harris, T. (1969) *I'm OK, You're OK*, London: Arrow Books.

46 It is very rewarding breaking transactions in this way, I do recommend giving it a go.

47 National Audit Office, *op. cit.*

48 Schwarz, N., Song, H., & Xu, J. (2009) When thinking is difficult: Metacognitive experiences as information, in M. Wänke (ed.) *The Social Psychology of Consumer Behavior*, New York: Psychology Press.

49 Kalher (1974), modified by Ian Stewart, taken from Stewart, I. (1996) *Developing Transactional Analysis Counselling*, London: Sage.

50 Carmon, Z. & Ariely, D. (2000) Focusing on the forgone: How value can appear so different to buyers and sellers, *Journal of Consumer Research*, 27(3): 360–70.

51 National Audit Office, *op. cit.*

42 Daily Telegraph (2009) Cut the TV licence fee by £5.50, says the BBC Chairman, *Daily Telegraph*, September 10.

53 www.bbc.co.uk/bbctrust/assets/files/pdf/news/2009/ipsos_mori_background.pdf.

54 *Daily Telegraph*, September 16, 2009.

55 *Digital Britain: Attitudes to supporting non-BBC regional news from the TV licence fee*, Interim Summary Report prepared for the Department of Culture Media and Sport, Sept 2009 (www.culture.gov.uk/images/publications/TNS-BMRB_interimsummaryreport.pdf).

56 *Ibid.*

57 Stanovich, K. (2009) *The Psychology of Rational Thought: What Intelligence Tests Miss*, New Haven, CT: Yale University Press.

58 Pervin, L.A. & John, O.P. (eds) *Handbook of Personality: Theory and Research*, 2nd edn, New York: Guilford Press; Shoda, Y., Mischel, W., & Wright, J.C. (1994) Intra-individual stability in the organization and patterning of behavior: Incorporating psychological situations into the idiographic analysis of personality, *Journal of Personality and Social Psychology*, 67: 674–87.

Chapter 6

1 Libet, B., Gleason, C.A., Wright, E.W., & Pearl, D.K. (1983) Time of conscious intention to act in relation to onset of cerebral activity (readiness-potential): The unconscious initiation of a freely voluntary act, *Brain*, 106(3): 623–42.

2 www.newscientist.com/article/dn13658-brain-scanner-predicts-your-future-moves.html?feedId=online-news_rss20.

3 Gladwell, *op. cit.*, p72.

4 Georgellis, Y. cited in Happiness "immune to life events," http://news.bbc.co.uk/1/hi/health/7502443.stm.

5 Damasio, *op. cit.*, p67.

6 Lieberman, D. (2007) *You Can Read Anyone: Never Be Fooled, Lied to, or Taken Advantage of Again*, Viter Press, p. 35.

Chapter 7

1 http://en.wikipedia.org/wiki/National_Socialist_German_ Workers_Party.

2 www.quackmedicine.com/. An analysis of nineteenth-century "quacks" and their success with customers provides many interesting lessons for organizations beyond the influence of groups, for example the manipulation of unconscious mood (entertainment) to increase susceptibility to influence and not letting a product's inherent lack of benefit stand in the way of people's willingness to endow it with one. We all like to think we're smarter than that these days, but sales of alternative medicines and market research might suggest otherwise.

3 Tanner, R.J., Ferraro, R., Chartrand, T.L., Bettman, J.R., & Van Baaren, R. (2008) Of chameleons and consumption: The impact of mimicry on choice and preferences, *Journal of Consumer Research*, April.

4 Berns, G., Capra, M., Moore, S., & Noussai, C. (2009) Neural Mechanisms of Social Influence in Consumer Decisions, *Organizational Behavior and Human Decision Processes*, 110(2): 152–9.

5 *Red Bull: The Anti-Brand Brand*, www.redbull.com/images/historysection/pdf/3/RB_Case_Study_London_Business_School0904.pdf; Wipperfürth, A., *Speed-in-a-Can: The Red Bull Story*, http://experiencethemessage.typepad.com/blog/files/Speed_In_a_Can.pdf.

6 www.upi.com/Top_News/2009/09/15/Swedish-stores-ban-Red-Bull-sales-to-kids/UPI-25571253062930/.

7 Asch, S.E. (1951) Effects of group pressure upon the modification and distor-

tion of judgment, in H. Guetzkow (ed.), *Groups, Leadership and Men*, New York: Carnegie Press.

8   http://news.cnet.com/8301-13579_3-10245339-37.html.
9   Stoner, J.A., Comparison of individual and group decisions involving risk, unpublished thesis, MIT, cited in Myers, D. G. & Lamm, H. (1975) The polarizing effect of group discussion, *American Scientist*, 63: 297–303.
10 Greenwald, A. (1968) Cognitive learning, cognitive response to persuasion, and attitude change, in A.G. Greenwald, T.C. Brock, & T.M. Ostrom (eds), *Psychological Foundations of Attitudes*, New York: Academic Press.
11 Vinokur, A. & Burnstein, E. (1974) The effects of partially shared persuasive arguments on group induced shifts: A group problem-solving approach, *Journal of Persuasion and Social Psychology*, 29: 305–15.
12 Weaver, K., Garcia, M., Schwarz, N., & Miller, D. (2007) Inferring the popularity of an opinion from its familiarity: A repetitive voice can sound like a chorus, *Journal of Personality and Social Psychology*, 92(5): 821–33.
13 Wegner, *op. cit.*, pp 180–9.
14 www.avguide.com/forums/blind-listening-tests-are-flawed-editorial.
15 Underhill, *op. cit.*
16 Beaman, A.L., Diener, E., & Klentz, B. (1979) Self-awareness and transgression in children: Two field studies, *Journal of Personality and Social Psychology*, 37: 1835–46.
17 Wicklund, R.A. & Duval, S. (1971) Opinion change and performance facilitation as a result of objective self awareness, *Journal of Experimental Social Psychology*, 7: 319–42.
18 Diener, E. & Wallbomm, M. (1976) Effects of self awareness on anti-normative behaviour, *Journal of Research in Personality*, 10: 107–11.
19 De Amici, D., Klersy, C., Ramajoli, F., & Brustia, L. The awareness of being observed changes the patient's psychological well-being in anesthesia, *Anesthesia & Analgesia*, 90(3): 739–41.
20 More recent reviews of the data have proposed that information feedback and financial reward may have accounted for the differences in behavior (see Parsons, H.M. (1974) What happened at Hawthorne?, *Science*, 183: 922–32).
21 Gifford, R. (1988) Light, decor, arousal, comfort, and communication, *Journal of Environmental Psychology*, 8: 177–89.
22 Wikipedia (2008) The Hawthorne Effect, www.wikipedia.com.
23 Sauer, A. (2002) Consignia, Royal f*%# up, www.brand channel.com/features_profile.asp?pr_id=76.
24 Pendergrast, *op. cit.*

Chapter 8

1   Greene, *op. cit.*
2   http://online.wsj.com/article/SB121555041646936817.html.
3   www.timesonline.co.uk/tol/news/uk/article533842.ece.
4   Wilson, R.D., Gilbert, D.T., & Centerbar, D.B. (2002) Making sense: The causes of emotional evanescence, in J. Carillo & I. Brocas (eds), *Economics and Psychology*, Oxford: Oxford University Press.
5   Gilbert, D.T., Pinel, E.C., Wilson, T.D., Blumberg, S.J., & Wheatley, T.P. (1998) Immune neglect: A source of durability bias in affective forecasting, *Journal of Personality and Social Psychology*, 75: 617–38.
6   Wilson, T.D., Wheatley, T., Meyers, J.M., Gilbert, D.T., & Axsom, D. (2000)

Focalism: A source of durability bias in affective forecasting, *Journal of Personality and Social Psychology*, 78(5): 821–36.

7 Kahneman, D. & Miller, D.T. (1986) Norm theory: Comparing reality to its alternatives, *Psychological Review*, 93: 136–53.

8 Zajonc, R.B. (1968) Attitudinal effects of mere exposure, *Journal of Personality and Social Psychology Monographs*, 9(2, Part 2): 1–27.

9 Song, H. & Schwarz, N. (2008) If it's hard to read, it's hard to do: Processing fluency affects effort prediction and motivation, *Psychological Science*, 19(10): 986–8.

10 Winkielman, P. & Fazendeiro, T.A. (2003) The role of conceptual fluency in preference and memory, working paper, Department of Psychology, University of California, San Diego.

11 Labroo, A.A., Dhar, R., & Schwarz, N. (2008) Of frog wines and frowning watches: Semantic priming, perceptual fluency, and brand evaluation, *Journal of Consumer Research*, 34.

12 Alter, A.L. & Oppenheimer, D.M. (2006) Predicting short-term stock fluctuations by using processing fluency, *Proceedings of the National Academy of Sciences*, 103(24): 9369–72.

13 Pelham, B.W., Mirenberg, M.C., & Jones, J.T., Why Susie sells seashells by the seashore: Implicit egotism and major life decisions, www.stat.columbia.edu/~gelman/stuff_for_blog/susie.pdf.

14 www.youtube.com/watch?v=9gUJ5UBw2n8&feature=channel_page.

Chapter 9

1 Hopkins, C. (1923) *Scientific Advertising*, New York: McGraw-Hill.

2 Goldstein, Martin, & Caldini, *op. cit.*; University of Nottingham (2009) Saying sorry really does cost nothing, *ScienceDaily*, September 23. Retrieved September 28, 2009, from www.sciencedaily.com/releases/2009/09/090923105815.htm.

3 www.wired.co.uk/wired-magazine/archive/2010/04/features/work-smarter-inditex.aspx.

4 http://money.cnn.com/galleries/2008/fortune/0803/gallery.jobsqna.fortune/index.html.

Epilogue

1 http://online.versoadvertising.com/verso/VersoSurveyDBWPresentation.html.

INDEX

ACKNOWLEDGMENTS

I t is impossible to write a book about the importance of the unconscious mind and our inability to recognize its role in shaping our behavior without accepting that you will do a lousy job of acknowledging the people who have contributed to that book's development. Nevertheless, I reserve the right to take a well-intentioned stab at thanking the people who I feel have influenced this project in one form or another.

Jay Wright showed me by example that the secret to writing a book is to say that you're going to write one and then go ahead and do it. It sounds obvious, I know, but seeing someone I admire so much accomplish this almost certainly triggered an unconscious desire in me to copy him.

I consider myself most fortunate to have stumbled over Kevin Hogan's book *The Science of Influence* at Amazon, and even more fortunate to have been mentored by him subsequently. That my own book resides in a subdirectory on my computer beneath his name says much about his contribution to my starting, finishing, and getting it published. I'm also greatly honored that he has written the foreword.

Consumer.ology would almost certainly not have found its way into the world without the guidance and encouragement of Francis Bennett, whose involvement was further evidence of my good luck. When I asked my parents-in-law, Adam and Annabel Ridley, if they knew of anyone I could solicit publishing advice from, I hoped that they might be acquainted with someone who would share a few minutes of their time with me in a phone call. I could never have dreamed that they would put me in touch with someone who had such vast experience of the publishing industry and who would be so generous with his assistance. To have Francis on hand to answer any question has made the process of going from having written a book to having it published, one that I'm sure is fraught for most writers, positively enjoyable.

While I was writing *Consumer.ology*, the encouragement, first reading of chapters, and the "what's that word that's another way of saying" telephone helpline service from my father were incalculably valuable. Similarly, my immediate family made the space and allowances I needed to get on and write. Despite having only recently started school, my children, George and Martha, set a wonderful example by producing several books of their own far more quickly and with far less fuss than me (although, in my defense, their Puffle stories are considerably shorter).

Numerous other people have contributed to this project in ways too diverse to detail (and by being nonspecific there's less chance that I will demonstrably overlook aspects of their contributions): Stephen Barnes, David Barlow, April Braswell, Steve Chambers, Dean Chance, Duane Cunningham, Richard Graves, Bryan Griffiths, J.P. Harrop, John Ho, Catherine Rickwood, JJ Jallopy, Lynn Lane, Lisa McLellan, Rob Northrup, Darryl Pace, David Parnell, Mitch Rehaume, Bob Seymore, Hugh Terry, Nathan Whitehouse, and Michael Wright.

Nick Brealey, Erika Heilman, and Sally Lansdell had the gifts of recognizing what I wanted to say and helping me to express it better. It was usually easy for me to see why their advice was perceptive and beneficial, and on the occasions when I didn't appreciate it immediately this was invariably my failing not theirs.

Finally, to the clients who have employed me to help them or invited me to speak to their organizations, and the psychologists and neuroscientists who are exploring the complex world of the human mind and whose work I have referenced, thank you – this book wouldn't have been possible without you.